At the
Southern Table
with Paula Deen

By Paula Deen

At the
Southern Table

with Paula Deen

150 CLASSIC RECIPES TO SHARE WITH FAMILY AND FRIENDS

PDV

Paula Deen Ventures
2391 Downing Ave.
Thunderbolt, GA 31404

All rights reserved, including the right to reproduce this book or
portions thereof in any form whatsoever. For information, address
Paula Deen Ventures Subsidiary Rights Department, 2391 Downing Ave.,
Thunderbolt, GA 31404.

Library of Congress Cataloging-in-Publication data is available

ISBN: 978-1-943016-06-8

Paula Deen Ventures and colophon are registered trademarks of Paula Deen Ventures, Inc.

Follow Paula's social media channels to stay up to date on her comings and goings, get her
favorite recipes, and catch a glimpse of her everyday life.

For more delicious Southern recipes from Paula, visit *pauladeenmagazine.com* and subscribe
to *Cooking with Paula Deen* magazine. Every issue is chock-full of easy, tasty recipes and
plenty of Deen family fun.

Manufactured in the United States of America

22 21 20 19 18 17   0 9 8 7 6 5 4 3 2 1

This book is dedicated to
all who long to have their feet
under Mama's table again.

Standing, left to right: Michael's son Anthony, his wife, Ashley, and introducing their son, Bennett Rich Groover; Paula's older son, Jamie, and his wife, Brooke; Paula's younger son, Bobby, and his wife, Claudia.

Seated, left to right: Michael; Paula; Jamie and Brooke's children, Matthew and Jack; Paula's niece, Corrie; Aunt Peggy.

contents

CLASSIC PAIRINGS 75
Soups, Salads, and Sandwiches

SOUTHERN SIDES 107
Vegetables and More

CASSEROLES FOR A CROWD 131
One-Dish Dinners

SOMETHIN' SWEET 159
Desserts

FAMILY GATHERINGS 193
Family Meals

MENUS MADE SIMPLE 241
Meal Planner

Cooking from the Heart

My two biggest passions in life are my family and good old-fashioned, down-home Southern cooking. I'm fortunate to have been blessed with an abundance of both.

I learned how to cook from my mama and grandmamas, and my Aunt Peggy, but it never occurred to me that we were cooking and eating "Southern" food; it was simply, good food. Of course, after I got married and started a family of my own, my sons, Jamie and Bobby, grew up eating the same things I did.

In the mid-1980s, when I suddenly found myself a single mother with two children to support, I turned to the only thing at the time that I knew I could do well: cooking. When I started The Bag Lady in 1989, I made sack lunches and heat-and-eat dinners out of my home, and Jamie and Bobby went around to local businesses in Savannah selling the meals. Praise the Lord it was a success, and it started us all on the path to where we are today.

My boys and I spent a lot of years struggling, but I did my best to give them the same traditions and experiences as children that I'd had, the most important of which were home-cooked foods and family meals at the table. I have such strong memories of when I was a girl, around the dinner table with my brother and parents, and any other relatives or friends who may have popped in for a quick chat. If you were there at mealtime, you got fed. Even if it wasn't mealtime, visitors were always served iced tea and a little something to snack on. That's just the way Southern hospitality works.

We cooked and ate with the seasons, growing and harvesting fruits and veggies in our home garden, and canning and preserving as much as we could to tide us over as the months came and went. And even though nowadays you can get just about any food at any time of year in the grocery store, it'll never taste as good as if it was grown near where you live and cooked fresh.

Jamie and Bobby and my niece, Corrie, grew up learning these customs, and they are continuing these traditions with their own families. Our family has grown in other ways, as well. When I married Michael, his daughter, Michelle, and son, Anthony, became part of my family. They both have children, and between us, Michael and I have six grandsons! We are truly blessed.

When we're not all scattered to the winds with school, work, and other commitments, there is nothing in the world I love more than having all our children and grandchildren over to our house and cooking a meal for them. My kitchen is definitely my happy place, and all the goodies I whip up are my way of expressing love for my family and dear friends. After spending decades in the kitchen, cooking up treasured family favorites or trying out new meals for a change of pace, I have a collection of delicious, trustworthy, well-used recipes that I can always rely on to put smiles on my family's faces.

Because these recipes are inspired by my years of making everything from easy weeknight meals and Saturday morning breakfasts to dishes for a potluck or a more formal affair, there's a little bit of everything in this cookbook. Whether new or old, simple or elaborate, these meals and menus have been with me as I've celebrated the most festive and everyday occasions in my life, and I love that I get to invite you into my kitchen and share them with you.

My favorite way to start the day at the table is with a big, hearty breakfast, so I thought I'd start this cookbook the same way. Every good Southern cook needs a can't-fail recipe for grits, biscuits and gravy, and a breakfast casserole, plus some fun dishes like chicken and waffles and doughnuts for a little extra breakfast-table excitement.

Freshly baked breads are another must-have in the Southern kitchen, so I've included recipes for cornbread, hoecakes, hush puppies, and lots more breads to inspire you to get to baking so you can enjoy a warm treat in no time. For entertaining or an easy snack, I pull from my arsenal of delicious appetizers that always please a crowd and start the meal off right.

Some of my all-time favorite lunches are soups, salads, and sandwiches, and these recipes are anything but basic, ranging from burgers and chicken salad to gumbo and fruit salad. For dinner, you can't go wrong with a cheesy, creamy casserole and veggie or side dish. These are all worthy of company or just a night at home with the family. Last but certainly not least is dessert. My pies, cakes, cookies, and more are the perfect way to add a sweet finish to a wonderful mealtime together.

You can combine elements from each of these chapters to make a fabulous meal, but if you're looking for ready-made menus, I'm sharing some of my favorites. My menus for a family reunion, a harvest celebration meal, and a hearty soup supper will guide you through all the elements of serving these feasts without a hitch, plus you'll find six more menus for breakfasts, lunches, and dinners in the back of this cookbook just before the recipe index.

When it comes to these classic recipes that have proven themselves time and time again at countless get-togethers, holidays, church suppers, picnics, and barbecues—well, as the saying goes, "if it ain't broke, don't fix it." These recipes have been my faithful go-tos for years and have never let me down. It's my hope that these dishes that have filled my family with comfort and made memories for us all will inspire you to cook up the same traditions with your loved ones.

From my table to yours,

Rise and Shine

BREAKFAST

For generations, Southern cooks have been whipping up hearty morning meals, and there's nothing quite like a big bowl of grits or fluffy biscuits smothered in creamy gravy. With these classic recipes, I know you'll create wonderful memories of gathering around the table with your family to enjoy the most important meal of the day.

Spiced Buttermilk Doughnuts

Makes about 18

Whether you're a glaze fan or a sugar fan, you have both options in this recipe.

3¾ to 4 cups all-purpose flour

2 cups granulated sugar, divided

2 teaspoons baking powder

2½ teaspoons ground cinnamon, divided

1 teaspoon baking soda

½ teaspoon salt

¼ cup cold unsalted butter, cubed

½ cup whole buttermilk

2 large eggs

¼ cup apple juice

1 teaspoon vanilla extract

Vegetable oil, for frying

2 cups confectioners' sugar

5 tablespoons heavy whipping cream

1. In a large bowl, beat 3¾ cups flour, 1 cup granulated sugar, baking powder, 1½ teaspoons cinnamon, baking soda, and salt with a mixer at low speed until combined. Add butter, beating until mixture is crumbly, 1 to 2 minutes.

2. In a medium bowl, whisk together buttermilk, eggs, apple juice, and vanilla. Add buttermilk mixture to flour mixture, beating until a soft dough forms. If dough is sticky, add up to remaining ¼ cup flour.

3. Turn out dough onto a sheet of parchment paper sprinkled with flour, and knead until smooth. Sprinkle dough with flour, and top with another sheet of parchment paper. Roll dough to ½-inch thickness. Transfer parchment with dough to a large baking sheet, and freeze until top sheet of parchment can be easily removed, 20 to 30 minutes.

4. Line a large rimmed baking sheet with paper towels, and place a wire rack on top.

5. In a large Dutch oven, pour oil to a depth of 3 inches, and heat over medium-high heat until a deep-fry thermometer registers 350°.

6. Remove dough from freezer, and slide parchment paper onto work surface; remove top sheet of parchment. Using a 2¾-inch doughnut cutter dipped in flour, cut out doughnuts, reserving doughnut holes. Reroll scraps once, and cut again.

7. Using a slotted spoon or a metal spatula, carefully lower doughnuts and doughnut holes into hot oil, and fry in batches until golden brown, 1 to 2 minutes per side, turning once. Let drain on prepared rack. Let cool slightly.

8. In a small bowl, stir together remaining 1 cup granulated sugar and remaining 1 teaspoon cinnamon. In a medium bowl, whisk together confectioners' sugar and cream. Dredge warm doughnuts and doughnut holes in cinnamon sugar and cream glaze as desired. Return to rack, and let cool completely. Store in an airtight container for up to 2 days.

Southern Eggs Benedict

Makes 2 servings

Using biscuits instead of English muffins and country ham for Canadian bacon,
you can enjoy a down-South spin on this classic breakfast favorite.

7 thin slices country ham, halved
14 fresh thin to medium-thick asparagus spears, trimmed
1 tablespoon olive oil
2 large eggs, room temperature
1 cup water
1 (1.25-ounce) package hollandaise sauce mix
¼ cup butter
½ teaspoon dried tarragon
1 tablespoon whole-grain mustard
2 baked biscuits, halved and toasted

1. Preheat oven to 400°. Line a rimmed baking sheet with foil.
2. Wrap 1 piece of ham around each asparagus spear, and place on prepared pan. Drizzle with oil.
3. Bake for 5 minutes. Turn asparagus, and bake 5 minutes more. Remove from oven; reduce oven temperature to 325°.
4. Spray 2 (6-ounce) ovenproof ramekins with cooking spray. Place ramekins on a rimmed baking sheet. Crack one egg into each ramekin.
5. Bake until eggs are set, 12 to 14 minutes. Gently run a knife around edges of ramekins to release eggs.
6. Meanwhile, in a medium saucepan, whisk together 1 cup water and hollandaise mix until smooth. Add butter and tarragon, and bring to a boil over medium-high heat, stirring occasionally. Reduce heat, and simmer until sauce is thickened. Remove from heat, and stir in mustard.
7. Place biscuits, cut side up, on serving plates, and top with asparagus, eggs, and hollandaise. Serve immediately.

Brown Sugar Bacon

Makes about 4 servings

Some call bacon the candy of meats—this recipe makes good on that.

12 slices thick-cut applewood-smoked bacon
¼ cup honey mustard
½ cup firmly packed dark brown sugar

1. Preheat oven to 375°. Line a large rimmed baking sheet with foil. Place a wire rack on pan; spray rack with cooking spray.
2. Place bacon in a single layer on prepared rack. Brush bacon with mustard, and sprinkle with brown sugar, pressing gently to adhere.
3. Bake until browned, 25 to 30 minutes (bacon will crisp as it cools). Serve immediately.

Banana-Nut Oat Pancakes

Makes about 12

These aren't your typical Saturday-morning pancakes, but they might just become your new favorite.

¾ cup old-fashioned oats
½ cup whole buttermilk
¾ cup all-purpose flour
¼ cup sugar
2 teaspoons baking powder
½ teaspoon baking soda
½ teaspoon kosher salt
½ teaspoon ground cinnamon
2 large eggs
¾ cup whole milk
½ teaspoon vanilla extract
1 ripe banana, diced
¼ cup chopped pecans
Vanilla Maple Syrup (recipe
    follows)
Garnish: sliced bananas, chopped
    pecans

1. In a small bowl, stir together oats and buttermilk; let stand for 20 minutes.

2. In a large bowl, whisk together flour, sugar, baking powder, baking soda, salt, and cinnamon. In a medium bowl, whisk together eggs, milk, and vanilla. Stir egg mixture and oat mixture into flour mixture just until combined; fold in banana and pecans.

3. Spray a large griddle or nonstick skillet with cooking spray, and heat over medium heat. Cook batter by ½ cupfuls until edges are dry and bubbles form in center of pancakes, 3 to 4 minutes. Turn and cook until bottom is browned, 1 to 2 minutes more. Serve immediately with Vanilla Maple Syrup; garnish with bananas and pecans, if desired.

Vanilla Maple Syrup

Makes 1 cup

1 cup pure maple syrup
1 vanilla bean, split lengthwise,
    seeds scraped and reserved

1. In a small saucepan, heat maple syrup, vanilla bean, and reserved seeds over low heat, stirring occasionally, until very warm and fragrant (do not boil). Discard vanilla bean before serving.

Perfect Grits

Makes about 3½ cups

These act as a tasty canvas to create a grits masterpiece with your own combination of mix-ins.

4 cups water
1 cup stone-ground grits
1½ teaspoons kosher salt
½ teaspoon ground black
   pepper
Toppings: butter, shredded
   cheese, crumbled cooked
   bacon, chopped green onion

1. In a medium saucepan, bring 4 cups water to a boil over high heat. Whisk in grits, salt, and pepper. Reduce heat, and simmer, whisking occasionally, until grits are tender and liquid is absorbed, about 35 minutes. Serve with desired toppings.

Chicken Sausage Patties
Makes 8

Make these yummy patties when you're wanting to change up your morning breakfast menu.

1 **pound ground chicken**
2 **tablespoons chopped green onion**
1 **teaspoon fennel seeds, crushed**
1 **teaspoon rubbed sage**
½ **teaspoon kosher salt**
½ **teaspoon ground black pepper**
½ **teaspoon crushed red pepper**

1. In a large bowl, stir together all ingredients. Divide mixture into 8 portions, and shape each into a patty.
2. Spray a large nonstick skillet with cooking spray; heat over medium-high heat. Cook patties until browned and cooked through, about 5 minutes per side. Serve immediately.

Spicy Fried Chicken and Cornbread Waffles

Makes about 12 servings

*"Who knew two seemingly opposite foods could go so well together?
I like to serve this dish with boneless chicken breasts because they're easy to eat,
but it's nice to also cook up a few drumsticks for folks who love dark meat."—Paula*

2 pounds boneless skin-on chicken breasts, cut into thirds
2 pounds skin-on chicken drumsticks
4 cups whole buttermilk
2 tablespoons Dijon mustard
1 tablespoon hot sauce
Canola oil, for frying
4 cups all-purpose flour
3 tablespoons kosher salt
1 teaspoon ground black pepper
½ teaspoon ground red pepper
Cornbread Waffles (recipe follows)
Maple syrup

1. In a large heavy-duty resealable plastic bag, combine chicken, buttermilk, mustard, and hot sauce. Seal bag, tossing well to combine; refrigerate for at least 2 hours or up to overnight.

2. Preheat oven to 350°. Spray a wire rack with cooking spray; place rack on a rimmed baking sheet.

3. Fill a large Dutch oven halfway with oil, and heat over medium-high heat until a deep-fry thermometer registers 350°.

4. In a shallow dish, whisk together flour, salt, and peppers. Remove chicken from bag, discarding marinade. Dredge chicken in flour mixture, shaking off excess.

5. Fry chicken in batches, turning occasionally, until golden brown on all sides, about 10 minutes, adjusting heat as needed to maintain oil temperature of 350°. Place chicken on prepared rack.

6. Bake until a meat thermometer inserted in thickest portion registers 165°, 10 to 15 minutes. Serve immediately with Cornbread Waffles and maple syrup.

Cornbread Waffles

Makes about 14

2 cups plain stone-ground cornmeal
2 cups all-purpose flour
4 teaspoons baking powder
2 teaspoons kosher salt
1 teaspoon baking soda
3 cups whole buttermilk
½ cup unsalted butter, melted
2 large eggs

1. Preheat oven to 200°. Place a wire rack on a large rimmed baking sheet. Spray a waffle iron with cooking spray, and heat according to manufacturer's instructions.

2. In a large bowl, whisk together cornmeal, flour, baking powder, salt, and baking soda. In another large bowl, whisk together buttermilk, melted butter, and eggs. Slowly stir buttermilk mixture into cornmeal mixture just until combined.

3. Cook batter by ⅓ cupfuls until golden brown and crisp, about 5 minutes. Transfer cooked waffle to wire rack, and keep warm in oven while cooking remaining batter.

Ham, Egg, and Cheese Biscuit Bites

Makes 16

These easy creations are a filling, portable breakfast.

2 (16.3-ounce) cans refrigerated buttermilk biscuits
1 tablespoon olive oil
½ cup chopped ham
¼ cup minced red bell pepper
2 tablespoons minced green onion
7 large eggs
½ teaspoon salt
¼ teaspoon ground black pepper
2½ cups shredded Cheddar cheese, divided

1. Preheat oven to 375°.
2. Press biscuits into bottom and up sides of 16 muffin cups.
3. In a large nonstick skillet, heat oil over medium heat. Add ham, bell pepper, and green onion; cook, stirring occasionally, for 5 minutes.
4. In a large bowl, whisk together eggs, salt, and pepper. Add eggs and 1½ cups cheese to skillet; cook, stirring frequently, until eggs are almost set. Divide egg mixture among biscuit cups, and sprinkle with ½ cup cheese.
5. Bake until golden brown, 12 to 15 minutes. Sprinkle with remaining ½ cup cheese; bake 2 minutes more. Let cool in pan for 5 minutes; serve warm.

Baked Eggs in Hash Brown Cups

Makes 6

This is a great dish to make for a Sunday morning at home or a brunch party.

3 cups frozen shredded hash brown potatoes, thawed
½ cup grated fresh Parmesan cheese
½ teaspoon kosher salt, divided
¼ teaspoon ground black pepper, divided
6 large eggs
Garnish: chopped fresh thyme

1. Preheat oven to 350°. Spray a 6-cup jumbo muffin pan with baking spray with flour.
2. In a large bowl, stir together hash browns, cheese, ¼ teaspoon salt, and ⅛ teaspoon pepper. Press ½ cup mixture into bottom and up sides of prepared muffin cups.
3. Bake until golden brown, about 1 hour. Let cool for 10 minutes.
4. Crack eggs into cups. Sprinkle with remaining ¼ teaspoon salt and remaining ⅛ teaspoon pepper.
5. Bake until desired degree of doneness, about 12 minutes for over-medium yolks. Garnish with thyme, if desired. Serve immediately.

Paula gathers fresh eggs daily from her chicken coop, the Chick Inn.

Pimiento Cheese Omelet

Makes 1 serving

Eggs made fluffy by heavy whipping cream are kicked up a notch with pimiento cheese and green onion. It's so good you'll want seconds.

2 large eggs

1 tablespoon heavy whipping cream

¼ teaspoon kosher salt

1 tablespoon unsalted butter

⅓ cup Pimiento Cheese (recipe on page 64)

2 tablespoons chopped green onion

Toppings: chopped green onion, diced pimientos, shredded Cheddar cheese

1. In a medium bowl, whisk together eggs, cream, and salt.

2. In a small nonstick skillet, melt butter over medium heat. Add egg mixture; cook, without stirring, until edges are set. Using a spatula, lift up cooked edges so that uncooked portion flows underneath; cook until center is just set. Spread Pimiento Cheese and green onion onto one side of eggs. Let stand for 10 seconds. Using a spatula, fold opposite side of eggs over to enclose filling. Invert omelet onto a serving plate. Serve immediately with desired toppings.

—————— **KITCHEN TIP** ——————

If you're short on time, feel free to use store-bought pimiento cheese.

Apricot Honey Buns

Makes 9

These sticky buns are a warm breakfast treat the whole family will love.

¼ cup warm water (105° to 110°)
1 teaspoon active dry yeast
4 cups self-rising flour
½ cup cold unsalted butter, cubed
¾ cup whole buttermilk
½ cup honey, divided
1 cup apricot preserves
½ cup butter, softened and divided
1 cup toasted sliced almonds

1. Preheat oven to 400°. Line a 9-inch square baking pan with foil, letting excess extend over sides of pan. Spray foil with cooking spray.
2. In a small bowl, stir together ¼ cup warm water and yeast; let stand until mixture is foamy, about 5 minutes.
3. In a large bowl, toss together flour and cold butter. Using a pastry blender, cut in butter until mixture is crumbly. Refrigerate for 10 minutes.
4. In a small bowl, stir together buttermilk and ¼ cup honey. Stir buttermilk mixture and yeast mixture into flour mixture just until dry ingredients are moistened.
5. Turn out dough onto a lightly floured surface, and knead 3 to 4 times, adding just enough additional flour to keep from sticking. Roll dough to a 14x12-inch rectangle.
6. In a small bowl, stir together preserves and ¼ cup softened butter; spread mixture onto dough. Starting at one long side, roll up dough into a log, pressing edges to seal. Cut dough into 9 (1½-inch-thick) slices.
7. In a small saucepan, cook remaining ¼ cup honey and remaining ¼ cup softened butter over low heat, stirring frequently, until butter is melted. Pour honey mixture into prepared pan, and sprinkle with almonds. Place dough slices in pan on almonds.
8. Bake until golden brown and a wooden pick inserted in center comes out clean, 25 to 30 minutes. Let cool in pan for 5 minutes. Invert onto a serving plate, and gently remove foil; serve warm.

PB&J Waffles

Makes 12

Bring the flavors of this classic sandwich to your breakfast table.

2¼ cups all-purpose flour
4 teaspoons baking powder
¼ teaspoon kosher salt
2 cups whole milk
¾ cup creamy peanut butter
¼ cup canola oil
1½ tablespoons sugar
2 large eggs
Strawberry preserves
Chopped peanuts

1. Spray a waffle iron with cooking spray, and heat according to manufacturer's instructions.
2. In a large bowl, whisk together flour, baking powder, and salt. In a medium bowl, whisk together milk and peanut butter until smooth; whisk in oil, sugar, and eggs until well combined. Stir milk mixture into flour mixture just until combined.
3. Cook batter by ¼ cupfuls until lightly browned, 2 to 3 minutes. Serve immediately with strawberry preserves and peanuts.

Southern Biscuits and Peppered Sausage Gravy

Makes about 8 servings

Folding the dough before rolling and cutting is what makes the flaky layers in these biscuits so irresistibly good.

2½ cups self-rising flour

2 tablespoons sugar

1¼ teaspoons kosher salt

¾ cup cold unsalted butter, cubed

1 cup cold whole buttermilk

2 tablespoons unsalted butter, melted

Peppered Sausage Gravy (recipe follows)

1. Preheat oven to 425°. Line a large rimmed baking sheet with parchment paper.

2. In a large bowl, whisk together flour, sugar, and salt. Using a pastry blender, cut in cold butter until mixture is crumbly. Stir in buttermilk just until combined.

3. Turn out dough onto a heavily floured surface. Shape dough into a flat log, and fold into thirds like a letter. Roll to a 10x8-inch rectangle. Using a lightly floured 3-inch round cutter, cut dough (do not twist cutter). Place biscuits 2 inches apart on prepared pan; gently reroll scraps and cut. Brush with melted butter.

4. Bake until golden brown, 12 to 14 minutes. Serve immediately with Peppered Sausage Gravy.

Peppered Sausage Gravy

Makes about 4½ cups

1 pound ground pork breakfast sausage

⅓ cup all-purpose flour

3 cups whole milk

½ cup heavy whipping cream

1½ teaspoons kosher salt

¼ teaspoon ground black pepper

1. In a large skillet, cook sausage over medium-high heat until browned and crumbly, about 10 minutes. Sprinkle flour onto sausage, and stir until well combined. Gradually whisk in milk, cream, salt, and pepper, and bring to a boil over medium heat. Reduce heat, and simmer, stirring frequently, until thickened, about 10 minutes. Serve immediately.

KITCHEN TIP

"More times than not, I add a pinch of garlic powder to my sausage gravy. It gives the gravy a great savory flavor. If you're a garlic fan, I promise you'll love it."—Paula

---

Cheesy Sausage and Greens Casserole

Makes 6 servings

This is a hearty all-in-one breakfast dish.

1 pound ground pork breakfast sausage

1 (5-ounce) bag fresh spinach, chopped

1½ cups shredded sharp white Cheddar cheese, divided

1 cup shredded smoked Gouda cheese

1⅓ cups self-rising flour

1 teaspoon salt

¼ teaspoon crushed red pepper

1½ cups whole milk

6 large eggs

½ cup oil-packed sun-dried tomatoes, drained and chopped

Garnish: chopped fresh basil

1. Preheat oven to 350°. Spray a shallow 3-quart baking dish with cooking spray.

2. In a medium skillet, cook sausage over medium heat until browned and crumbly; drain.

3. Layer spinach, sausage, 1 cup Cheddar, and Gouda in prepared pan. In a medium bowl, whisk together flour, salt, and red pepper. Whisk in milk and eggs until combined. Pour onto spinach mixture, and top with tomatoes and remaining ½ cup Cheddar.

4. Bake until center is set, 25 to 30 minutes. Let stand for 5 minutes before serving. Garnish with basil, if desired.

Baked Apple Pie French Toast

Makes 6 servings

"I love dessert for breakfast!"—Paula

6 tablespoons butter, divided
6 cups sliced Gala apples
1 tablespoon fresh lemon juice
1¼ teaspoons apple pie spice, divided
¾ pound French bread, cut into ½-inch-thick slices
8 large eggs
2 cups whole milk
⅔ cup granulated sugar
2 teaspoons vanilla extract
⅛ teaspoon salt
Confectioners' sugar
Maple syrup

1. In a large skillet, melt 2 tablespoons butter over medium heat. Add apples, and cook until tender, about 8 minutes. Remove from heat; stir in lemon juice and 1 teaspoon pie spice.

2. Spray a 13x9-inch baking dish with cooking spray.

3. Arrange half of bread in bottom of prepared pan, overlapping slices as necessary. Spread apples onto bread; top with remaining bread. In a large bowl, whisk together eggs, milk, granulated sugar, vanilla, and salt. Pour onto bread; gently press with a spatula. Cover and refrigerate for at least 8 hours or up to overnight.

4. Preheat oven to 350°. Uncover casserole, and let stand at room temperature for 30 minutes.

5. In a small microwave-safe bowl, melt remaining 4 tablespoons butter with remaining ¼ teaspoon pie spice; drizzle onto bread.

6. Bake until golden brown and center is set, 35 to 40 minutes. Sprinkle with confectioners' sugar; serve with maple syrup.

All Floured Up

BREADS AND BAKING

There's nothing quite like the smell of bread baking in the oven to welcome folks into your home. From muffins in the morning and hot-from-the oven yeast rolls at dinnertime to skillet cornbread and quick breads any time of day, it's hard to beat homemade bread. I hope you enjoy baking up these Southern favorites.

Blueberry Streusel Muffins

Makes 18

Streusel comes from the German word streuen, *meaning "to sprinkle."*

Topping:
- ½ cup all-purpose flour
- ½ cup sugar
- 1 teaspoon ground cinnamon
- 5 tablespoons cold butter, cubed
- ⅔ cup chopped pecans

Muffins:
- 3 cups all-purpose flour
- 1 cup sugar
- 1 tablespoon baking powder
- ½ teaspoon baking soda
- ¼ teaspoon salt
- 2 large eggs
- ¾ cup whole milk
- ¾ cup sour cream
- ½ cup butter, melted and cooled
- 1½ cups fresh blueberries

1. Preheat oven to 350°. Spray 18 muffin cups with baking spray with flour.

2. For topping: In a small bowl, whisk together flour, sugar, and cinnamon. Using a pastry blender, cut in butter until mixture is crumbly. Stir in pecans.

3. For muffins: In a large bowl, whisk together flour, sugar, baking powder, baking soda, and salt. In a small bowl, whisk together eggs, milk, sour cream, and melted butter. Stir egg mixture into flour mixture just until combined; gently fold in blueberries. Spoon batter into prepared muffin cups, filling two-thirds full; sprinkle with topping.

4. Bake until a wooden pick inserted in center comes out clean, about 18 minutes. Let cool in pan for 10 minutes; serve warm.

——————————————— **KITCHEN TIP** ———————————————

Raspberries, blackberries, chopped strawberries,
or chopped cherries can be used in place of blueberries.

Corn Fritters

Makes about 30

Fritters can be kept warm in a 200° oven for up to 20 minutes after frying.

2 tablespoons butter
1 cup fresh or thawed frozen corn kernels
1 cup minced onion
1½ cups self-rising cornmeal mix
½ cup all-purpose flour
½ teaspoon salt
1 cup whole buttermilk
2 large eggs
1 cup shredded fontina cheese
Vegetable oil, for frying

1. In a medium skillet, melt butter over medium heat. Add corn and onion; cook, stirring occasionally, until onion is tender, about 5 minutes.

2. In a large bowl, whisk together cornmeal mix, flour, and salt. In a small bowl, whisk together buttermilk and eggs. Stir buttermilk mixture into flour mixture just until dry ingredients are moistened. Stir in cheese and onion mixture.

3. In a Dutch oven, pour oil to a depth of 3 inches, and heat over medium-high heat until a deep-fry thermometer registers 360°. Drop batter by heaping tablespoonfuls into hot oil; fry until golden brown, 2 to 3 minutes per side. Let drain on paper towels; serve warm.

Blue Cheese and Sage Muffins

Makes 24

These mini muffins pack a big flavor punch, and they come together in a snap.

2 cups self-rising flour
½ cup cold butter, cubed
½ cup crumbled blue cheese
1 teaspoon ground sage
1 (8-ounce) container sour cream
¼ cup whole milk

1. Preheat oven to 400°. Spray 24 miniature muffin cups with cooking spray.

2. In a large bowl, place flour. Using a pastry blender, cut in butter until mixture is crumbly. Stir in cheese and sage. Make a well in center of flour mixture.

3. In a small bowl, whisk together sour cream and milk. Stir sour cream mixture into flour mixture just until combined. Spoon batter into prepared muffin cups.

4. Bake until golden brown, about 10 minutes. Let cool in pans for 5 minutes; serve warm.

Orange Cream Cheese Rolls

Makes 24

These smooth, rich rolls with a touch of citrus are a delicious morning treat.

Dough:
1½ cups warm whole milk
    (105° to 110°)
2   (0.25-ounce) packages active
    dry yeast
1   cup sugar
¾   cup butter, melted
1   tablespoon orange zest
½   cup fresh orange juice
3   large eggs
1   teaspoon salt
8 to 9 cups bread flour, divided

Filling:
1   (8-ounce) package cream
    cheese, softened
¼   cup orange marmalade
2   tablespoons sugar
½   cup chopped pecans

Glaze:
2   cups confectioners' sugar
¼   cup fresh orange juice

1. For dough: In a small bowl, stir together warm milk and yeast; let stand until mixture is foamy, about 5 minutes.

2. In a large bowl, beat sugar, melted butter, orange zest and juice, eggs, and salt with a mixer at medium-low speed until combined. Add yeast mixture, beating until combined. Gradually add 7 cups bread flour, beating until smooth. Gradually add enough remaining bread flour to make a soft dough.

3. Turn out dough onto a lightly floured surface, and knead until smooth and elastic, 6 to 8 minutes. Spray a large bowl with cooking spray. Place dough in bowl, turning to grease top. Cover and let rise in a warm, draft-free place (75°) until doubled in size, about 1 hour.

4. Spray 2 (10-inch) round cake pans with cooking spray.

5. For filling: In a small bowl, stir together all ingredients until well combined.

6. On a lightly floured surface, roll dough to a 24x12-inch rectangle. Spread filling onto dough, leaving a ½-inch border on all sides. Starting at one long side, roll dough into a log, pinching seams to seal. Using a serrated knife, cut dough into 24 (1-inch-thick) slices. Place 12 slices, cut side down, in each prepared pan. Cover and let rise in a warm, draft-free place (75°) until doubled in size, about 1 hour.

7. Preheat oven to 350°.

8. Bake until golden brown, 20 to 25 minutes. Let cool in pans for 10 minutes.

9. For glaze: In a small bowl, whisk together all ingredients until smooth; drizzle onto warm rolls; serve immediately.

Corn Sticks

Makes about 18

Corn sticks are a fun alternative to a classic pan of cornbread.

¼ cup plus 2 tablespoons vegetable oil, divided
1½ cups plain yellow cornmeal
¼ cup all-purpose flour
3 tablespoons sugar
1 teaspoon baking soda
½ teaspoon baking powder
½ teaspoon salt
1 cup whole buttermilk
1 large egg

1. Preheat oven to 425°. Brush ¼ cup oil into wells of cast-iron corn stick pans, and place pans in oven to preheat.

2. In a large bowl, whisk together cornmeal, flour, sugar, baking soda, baking powder, and salt. In a small bowl, whisk together buttermilk, egg, and remaining 2 tablespoons oil. Stir buttermilk mixture into cornmeal mixture just until combined. Spoon batter into hot pans, filling wells three-fourths full.

3. Bake until golden brown, 8 to 10 minutes. Let cool in pan for 5 minutes; serve warm.

Creamed Corn Cornbread

Makes 1 (12-inch) skillet

Melty cheese and creamed corn create a sizzling skillet of golden cornbread that begs to be slathered in butter.

⅓ cup plus 3 tablespoons vegetable oil, divided
2 cups plain yellow cornmeal
1 cup all-purpose flour
1 tablespoon sugar
2 teaspoons baking powder
½ teaspoon baking soda
½ teaspoon salt
1 (15-ounce) can cream-style corn
1 cup whole buttermilk
3 large eggs
1 cup shredded Monterey Jack cheese

1. Preheat oven to 400°. Pour 3 tablespoons oil in a 12-inch cast-iron skillet, and place skillet in oven to preheat.

2. In a large bowl, whisk together cornmeal, flour, sugar, baking powder, baking soda, and salt. In a medium bowl, whisk together corn, buttermilk, eggs, and remaining ⅓ cup oil. Stir corn mixture into cornmeal mixture just until combined; stir in cheese. Pour batter into hot skillet.

3. Bake until a wooden pick inserted in center comes out clean, about 25 minutes. Let cool in pan for 5 minutes; serve warm.

KITCHEN TIP

Oiling and preheating cast-iron pans ensures a crispy crust to your cornbread and corn sticks.

Cinnamon Roll
Biscuits, page 37

Cinnamon Roll Biscuits

Makes 8

"These beauties give you all the goodness of a sweet roll but without the work of making a yeast dough."—Paula

3 cups self-rising flour

2 tablespoons granulated sugar

½ cup cold butter, cut into pats

1¼ cups cold whole buttermilk

3 tablespoons butter, softened

¼ cup firmly packed light brown sugar

¾ teaspoon ground cinnamon

3 tablespoons butter, melted (optional)

2 cups confectioners' sugar

3 tablespoons whole milk

⅛ teaspoon salt

1. Preheat oven to 450°. Lightly spray a 10-inch cast-iron skillet with cooking spray.

2. In a large bowl, whisk together flour and granulated sugar. Using a pastry blender, cut in cold butter until mixture is crumbly. Gradually add buttermilk, stirring with a fork just until dry ingredients are moistened.

3. On a lightly floured surface, turn out dough, and lightly knead 5 times. Pat or gently roll dough to a 14x8-inch rectangle. Brush with softened butter. In a small bowl, stir together brown sugar and cinnamon; sprinkle onto buttered dough. Starting at one long side, roll up dough into a log. Cut roll into 8 (1¾-inch-thick) slices. Place slices cut side up in prepared pan.

4. Bake until golden brown, 15 to 18 minutes. Brush with melted butter, if desired.

5. In a medium bowl, whisk together confectioners' sugar, milk, and salt. For a thin glaze, drizzle onto biscuits while warm. For a thicker glaze, let biscuits cool for 30 to 45 minutes before glazing.

. VARIATION .
Sweet Potato Biscuits

Whisk together flour, ¼ cup firmly packed light brown sugar, and ¼ teaspoon ground nutmeg before cutting in butter. Stir in ¾ cup mashed cooked sweet potato before adding buttermilk, and decrease buttermilk to ½ cup plus 2 tablespoons. Pat dough to ¾-inch thickness, and cut using a 3-inch round cutter, gently rerolling and cutting scraps. Place biscuits on a parchment paper-lined baking sheet, and bake as directed.

Hoecakes

Makes about 16

"These signature delicacies are served to every guest at my restaurants The Lady & Sons and Paula Deen's Family Kitchen. It's my way of welcoming them to the table."—Paula

1 cup self-rising flour
1 cup self-rising cornmeal mix
1 tablespoon sugar
¾ cup whole buttermilk
⅓ cup plus 1 tablespoon water
¼ cup melted bacon drippings
    or vegetable oil
2 large eggs
Vegetable oil, for frying
Maple syrup

1. In a large bowl, whisk together flour, cornmeal mix, and sugar. In a small bowl, whisk together buttermilk, ⅓ cup plus 1 tablespoon water, drippings or oil, and eggs. Stir buttermilk mixture into flour mixture just until combined.

2. In a large skillet, pour oil to a depth of ¼ inch, and heat over medium heat until a deep-fry thermometer registers 350°.

3. Carefully drop batter by 2 tablespoonfuls into hot oil, and fry until brown and crisp on bottom. Turn and cook until brown and crisp on bottom. Let drain on paper towels; serve immediately with maple syrup.

Crispy Hush Puppies

Makes about 36

Legend has it these cornmeal bites were named when fishermen cooking up their catch of the day fried leftover batter to use as treats to silence the howls of their dogs begging for food.

Vegetable oil, for frying
2 cups plain yellow cornmeal
½ cup all-purpose flour
2½ teaspoons seasoned salt
2 teaspoons baking powder
1 teaspoon garlic powder
½ teaspoon ground black pepper
½ cup chopped green onion
1 jalapeño, seeded and minced
1½ cups whole buttermilk
1 large egg
2 teaspoons hot sauce

1. In a large Dutch oven, pour oil to a depth of 2 inches, and heat over medium heat until a deep-fry thermometer registers 350°.

2. In a large bowl, whisk together cornmeal, flour, seasoned salt, baking powder, garlic powder, and pepper; stir in green onion and jalapeño. In a small bowl, whisk together buttermilk, egg, and hot sauce. Stir buttermilk mixture into cornmeal mixture just until combined.

3. Carefully drop batter by tablespoonfuls into hot oil, and fry until golden brown, 3 to 4 minutes. Let drain on paper towels; serve immediately.

Cherry Danish

Makes 18

"I take advantage of convenience foods when possible, like frozen puff pastry for this recipe. There's no reason to make it from scratch when you have such a great product at your fingertips."—Paula

1 (17.3-ounce) package frozen puff pastry, thawed according to package directions
1½ cups canned cherry pie filling
2 teaspoons orange zest
⅛ teaspoon almond extract
½ (8-ounce) package cream cheese, softened
1 large egg
1 tablespoon water
Garnish: confectioners' sugar

1. Preheat oven to 425°. Line 2 large rimmed baking sheets with parchment paper.

2. Working with one pastry sheet at a time (keep remaining sheet refrigerated), unfold pastry sheet onto a lightly floured surface. Cut pastry sheet into thirds lengthwise and again in thirds crosswise (you should have 9 pieces of pastry). Place pastry pieces on prepared pan.

3. In a small bowl, stir together pie filling, zest, and extract. Spread about 1 teaspoon cream cheese onto pastry pieces to within ½ inch of edges. Spoon 1 tablespoon pie filling mixture onto cream cheese. Fold up edges of pastry to form a border, pressing lightly. In a small bowl, whisk together egg and 1 tablespoon water; lightly brush onto pastry edges. Repeat with remaining pastry, cream cheese, pie filling mixture, and egg wash.

4. Bake until edges are lightly browned, 11 to 13 minutes. Let cool completely on a wire rack. Garnish with confectioners' sugar, if desired. Store in an airtight container for up to 1 day.

. VARIATION .

Apple Danish

Substitute apple pie filling, 1 teaspoon lemon zest, and vanilla extract for cherry pie filling, orange zest, and almond extract. Assemble and bake as directed.

Cheese and Onion Dinner Rolls

Makes 18

If the thought of making yeast bread intimidates you, this recipe is a great place to start.

4 tablespoons vegetable oil, divided
1 cup minced onion
1½ cups warm whole milk (105° to 110°), divided
4 teaspoons sugar, divided
1 (0.25-ounce) package active dry yeast
1 large egg, lightly beaten
1 cup shredded sharp Cheddar cheese
1 teaspoon salt
4¾ cups bread flour
½ cup grated fresh Parmesan cheese

1. In a medium skillet, heat 2 tablespoons oil over medium heat. Add onion; cook, stirring frequently, until tender, about 5 minutes. Remove from heat, and let cool.

2. In a small bowl, stir together ½ cup warm milk, 1 teaspoon sugar, and yeast; let stand until mixture is foamy, about 5 minutes.

3. In a large bowl, stir together egg, Cheddar, salt, onion, yeast mixture, remaining 3 teaspoons sugar, remaining 1 cup warm milk, and remaining 2 tablespoons oil. Gradually stir in flour until a soft dough forms.

4. Turn out dough onto a lightly floured surface, and knead until smooth and elastic. Spray a large bowl with cooking spray. Place dough in bowl, turning to grease top. Loosely cover, and let rise in a warm, draft-free place (75°) until doubled in size, about 1 hour.

5. Punch dough down. Cover and let stand for 10 minutes.

6. On a lightly floured surface, divide dough in half; divide each half into 9 portions. Roll each portion into a ball. Spray 2 (9-inch) round cake pans with cooking spray; place 9 dough balls in each prepared pan. Cover and let rise in a warm, draft-free place (75°) until doubled in size, about 1 hour.

7. Preheat oven to 350°.

8. Sprinkle rolls with Parmesan. Bake until lightly browned, 15 to 18 minutes. Let cool in pans for 5 minutes; serve warm.

Morning Glory Muffins

Makes 24

The pineapple, apple, and carrot bring a lot of moisture to these muffins, so they'll stay fresh for several days.

3 cups all-purpose flour
1½ cups sugar
1½ teaspoons baking soda
1 teaspoon ground cinnamon
½ teaspoon salt
3 large eggs
¾ cup vegetable oil
1 (8-ounce) can crushed pineapple, drained
1 cup finely shredded Granny Smith apple
1 cup finely shredded carrot
1 cup chopped pecans
1 cup golden raisins

1. Preheat oven to 350°. Spray 2 (12-cup) muffin pans with cooking spray.

2. In a large bowl, whisk together flour, sugar, baking soda, cinnamon, and salt. In a small bowl, whisk together eggs and oil. Stir egg mixture into flour mixture just until combined. Fold in pineapple and all remaining ingredients just until combined. Spoon batter into prepared muffin cups.

3. Bake until a wooden pick inserted in center comes out clean, about 20 minutes. Let cool in pans for 5 minutes; serve warm.

Rosemary Cheese Straws

Makes about 48

Cheese straws are a quintessential Southern snack.
They're equally at home at backyard cookouts and bridal teas.

1 cup unsalted butter, softened
1 (16-ounce) package extra-sharp Cheddar cheese, shredded
2½ cups all-purpose flour
1 tablespoon minced fresh rosemary
½ teaspoon salt

1. Preheat oven to 300°. Line baking sheets with parchment paper.
2. In the bowl of a stand mixer fitted with the paddle attachment, beat butter at medium speed until creamy. Add cheese, beating until combined.
3. In a medium bowl, whisk together flour, rosemary, and salt. Gradually add flour mixture to butter mixture, beating until combined. Using a cookie press or a pastry bag fitted with a large star tip, pipe cheese straws to desired length on prepared pans.
4. Bake until bottom of straws are lightly browned, about 20 minutes. Let cool on pans for 5 minutes. Remove from pans, and let cool completely on wire racks. Store in an airtight container for up to 1 week.

. VARIATION .
Spicy Pecan Cheese Wafers

Omit rosemary, and add 1½ cups finely chopped pecans and
1 teaspoon ground red pepper to dough. Roll dough into 1-inch balls,
and gently flatten with the bottom of a glass that's been lightly dipped in flour.
Bake as directed.

Sweet Potato Cranberry Scones

Makes 24

These not-too-sweet pastries are great for breakfast or as an afternoon snack.

4 cups all-purpose flour
½ cup granulated sugar
4 teaspoons baking powder
1½ teaspoons salt
1½ teaspoons ground cinnamon
1 teaspoon baking soda
¼ teaspoon ground nutmeg
¾ cup cold unsalted butter, cubed
1½ cups mashed cooked sweet potato
⅔ cup dried cranberries
½ cup whole buttermilk
1 large egg
1 cup confectioners' sugar
1 cup maple syrup

1. Preheat oven to 425°. Line baking sheets with parchment paper.
2. In a large bowl, whisk together flour, granulated sugar, baking powder, salt, cinnamon, baking soda, and nutmeg. Using a pastry blender, cut in butter until mixture is crumbly. Cut in sweet potato until well combined; stir in cranberries.
3. In a small bowl, whisk together buttermilk and egg. Gently stir buttermilk mixture into flour mixture just until combined (dough will be sticky).
4. Turn out dough onto a lightly floured surface, and roll to ½-inch thickness. Cut dough into 24 wedges, and place on prepared pans.
5. Bake until golden brown, 10 to 12 minutes. Let cool on pans for 5 minutes. Remove from pans, and let cool for 30 minutes on wire racks.
6. In a small bowl, whisk together confectioners' sugar and maple syrup; drizzle onto scones. Store in an airtight container for up to 2 days.

Strawberry Pecan Mini Loaves

Makes 3 (5½-inch) loaves

This bread is a winner with its sweet, bright berries.

2 cups self-rising flour
¾ cup plus 3 teaspoons sugar, divided
⅓ cup toasted finely chopped pecans
¾ cup whole milk
2 large eggs
2 tablespoons unsalted butter, melted
½ teaspoon lemon zest
1 cup chopped fresh strawberries

1. Preheat oven to 350°. Lightly spray 3 (5½x3-inch) loaf pans with baking spray with flour.
2. In a large bowl, whisk together flour, ¾ cup sugar, and pecans; make a well in center of dry ingredients. In a small bowl, whisk together milk, eggs, melted butter, and zest. Stir milk mixture into flour mixture just until combined; gently stir in strawberries. Divide batter among prepared pans.
3. Bake until a wooden pick inserted in center comes out clean, about 25 minutes. Sprinkle hot loaves with remaining 3 teaspoons sugar. Let cool in pan for 10 minutes. Remove from pans, and let cool completely on a wire rack. Store in an airtight container for up to 3 days.

Ginger Walnut Pumpkin Bread

Makes 2 (9-inch) loaves

*This flavorful quick bread recipe makes two loaves and freezes well,
so you can enjoy one now and have another one on hand.*

Bread:
- 3½ cups all-purpose flour
- 3 cups granulated sugar
- 2 teaspoons baking soda
- 1 teaspoon baking powder
- ½ teaspoon salt
- ½ teaspoon ground cinnamon
- ¼ teaspoon ground nutmeg
- ¼ teaspoon ground cloves
- 1 cup chopped walnuts
- ½ cup chopped crystallized ginger
- 2½ cups canned pumpkin
- 4 large eggs
- ½ cup vegetable oil
- 2 tablespoons whole milk

Topping:
- 5 tablespoons unsalted butter, melted
- ⅔ cup all-purpose flour
- 3 tablespoons firmly packed light brown sugar
- 3 tablespoons old-fashioned oats
- ½ teaspoon ground cinnamon

1. Preheat oven to 350°. Spray 2 (9x5-inch) loaf pans with cooking spray.

2. For bread: In a large bowl, whisk together flour, sugar, baking soda, baking powder, salt, cinnamon, nutmeg, and cloves. In a small bowl, toss together 2 tablespoons flour mixture, walnuts, and ginger.

3. In another large bowl, whisk together pumpkin, eggs, oil, and milk. Stir pumpkin mixture into flour mixture just until combined; fold in walnut mixture. Divide batter between prepared pans.

4. For topping: In a small bowl, stir together all ingredients until well combined. Sprinkle onto batter in pans.

5. Bake until a wooden pick inserted in center comes out clean, 60 to 70 minutes, loosely covering with foil halfway through baking time to prevent excess browning. Let cool in pans for 10 minutes. Remove from pans, and let cool completely on a wire rack. Store in an airtight container for up to 3 days.

. VARIATION .
Rum Raisin Pumpkin Bread

In a small microwave-safe bowl, heat ¼ cup rum on high until hot,
20 to 30 seconds. Add 1 cup raisins to rum, cover, and let stand for 30 minutes.
Prepare batter as directed, omitting walnuts and ginger. Drain raisins, and fold
into batter; omit topping, if desired. Bake as directed.

Banana Bread

Makes 1 (9-inch) loaf

"The riper the banana, the better for this bread. Bananas that are on the verge of spoiling, with mostly black peels, are perfect."—Paula

2¼ cups all-purpose flour
1 cup sugar
1 teaspoon baking soda
1 teaspoon kosher salt
4 ripe bananas, mashed (about 2 cups)
½ cup unsalted butter, melted
2 large eggs
1 teaspoon vanilla extract

1. Preheat oven to 325°. Spray a 9x5-inch loaf pan with baking spray with flour.
2. In a large bowl, whisk together flour, sugar, baking soda, and salt. In a medium bowl, whisk together banana, melted butter, eggs, and vanilla. Stir banana mixture into flour mixture until combined. Spread batter into prepared pan.
3. Bake until a wooden pick inserted in center comes out clean, about 1 hour. Let cool in pan for 10 minutes. Remove from pan, and let cool completely on a wire rack. Store in an airtight container for up to 3 days.

Dutch Baby

Makes 1 (10-inch) pancake

This is a fun twist on breakfast pancakes. The best part is watching it puff up in the oven as it bakes.

¼ **cup butter**
¾ **cup whole milk**
3 **large eggs**
¾ **cup all-purpose flour**
2 **tablespoons granulated sugar**
1 **teaspoon lemon zest**
Garnish: confectioners' sugar

1. Preheat oven to 450°. Place butter in a 10-inch cast-iron skillet, and place skillet in oven to melt butter.

2. In the container of a blender, process milk and eggs until smooth. Add flour, granulated sugar, and zest; process until smooth. Pour batter into melted butter in hot skillet.

3. Bake until golden brown and set, 12 to 15 minutes. Serve immediately; garnish with confectioners' sugar, if desired.

Buttermilk Oat Bread

Makes 2 (8-inch) loaves

This hearty bread is great for sandwiches or toasted and spread with butter and jam for breakfast.

1½ cups old-fashioned oats, divided
1 cup boiling water
¼ cup warm whole milk (105° to 110°)
2 tablespoons plus 2 teaspoons honey, divided
2 teaspoons active dry yeast
1½ cups whole buttermilk
½ cup olive oil
1 tablespoon kosher salt
5 cups all-purpose flour
1 tablespoon water

1. In a small bowl, stir together 1¼ cups oats and 1 cup boiling water; let stand for 10 minutes.

2. In the bowl of a stand mixer fitted with the dough hook attachment, combine warm milk, 2 tablespoons honey, and yeast; let stand until mixture is foamy, about 10 minutes.

3. In a small bowl, whisk together buttermilk, oil, and salt. Add buttermilk mixture and oat mixture to yeast mixture, and beat at low speed until combined. Gradually add flour, beating until combined. Increase speed to medium, and beat until dough is smooth, about 10 minutes (dough will still be sticky).

4. Spray a large bowl with cooking spray. Place dough in bowl, turning to grease top. Cover and let stand in a warm, draft-free place (75°) until doubled in size, about 1 hour.

5. Spray 2 (8-inch) loaf pans with cooking spray. Turn out dough onto a lightly floured surface, and divide dough in half. Shape each half into an 8-inch loaf, and place in prepared pans.

6. In a small microwave-safe bowl, heat 1 tablespoon water with remaining 2 teaspoons honey until warm. Brush honey mixture onto loaves. Sprinkle with remaining ¼ cup oats. Cover and let stand in a warm, draft-free place (75°) for 30 minutes.

7. Preheat oven to 375°.

8. Bake until golden brown, about 1 hour. Let cool in pans for 5 minutes. Remove from pans, and let cool completely on wire racks. Store in an airtight container for up to 3 days.

A Few Bites

APPETIZERS AND SNACKS

It's always been my experience that people who come to my house bring their hearty appetites, whether I've invited them for a meal or a friend drops in to say hello. It's so nice to have a little something that you can make ahead or throw together quickly for people to nibble on while you sit and visit. Even if they tell you they're not hungry, trust me, they are. No one will pass up these small bites of homemade goodness.

Turnip Greens and Bacon Dip

Makes about 6 cups

Hearty turnip greens take the place of the traditional spinach in this creamy dip.

6 slices bacon, chopped
1 cup chopped yellow onion
1 tablespoon minced fresh
  garlic
1 (16-ounce) package chopped
  fresh turnip greens
2 cups chicken broth
2 cups water
1 dried chile pepper
1 tablespoon kosher salt
1 tablespoon sugar
1½ (8-ounce) packages cream
  cheese, softened
½ cup sour cream
½ cup mayonnaise
¼ teaspoon ground red pepper
2 cups shredded fontina cheese
Garnish: shaved Parmesan cheese

1. In a Dutch oven, cook bacon over medium heat until crisp. Remove bacon using a slotted spoon, and let drain on paper towels, reserving drippings in pot.

2. Add onion and garlic to drippings; cook, stirring occasionally, until tender, about 5 minutes. Add turnip greens in batches, cooking until wilted after each addition. Increase heat to medium-high, and stir in broth, 2 cups water, chile pepper, salt, and sugar. Cook, stirring occasionally, until greens are tender, about 20 minutes. Drain, and let cool. Discard chile pepper, and squeeze excess liquid from greens.

3. Preheat oven to 350°. Spray a 1½-quart baking dish with cooking spray.

4. In the work bowl of a food processor, pulse together greens mixture, cream cheese, sour cream, mayonnaise, and red pepper until combined.

5. In a large bowl, stir together greens mixture, fontina, and three-fourths of bacon. Spoon into prepared pan.

6. Bake until hot and bubbly, about 20 minutes. Top with remaining bacon before serving; garnish with Parmesan, if desired.

——————————— KITCHEN TIP ———————————

You can lighten this dip by using reduced-fat dairy products and mayonnaise
in place of their full-fat versions.

Spicy Sausage Balls

Makes 36

"Make these the next time you're stumped for a tailgating snack—there won't be any leftovers."—Paula

1 (16-ounce) package ground spicy pork breakfast sausage
2 (8-ounce) packages shredded Monterey Jack cheese
3 cups all-purpose baking mix
¾ cup minced red bell pepper
2 large eggs, lightly beaten
1 jalapeño, seeded and minced
2 tablespoons minced fresh cilantro
1 teaspoon ground cumin

1. Preheat oven to 350°. Line a large rimmed baking sheet with foil; spray foil with cooking spray.

2. In a large bowl, gently mix together all ingredients with your hands until well combined. Shape mixture into 2-inch balls, and place on prepared pan.

3. Bake until golden brown, about 25 minutes. Let cool on pan for 2 minutes; serve warm or at room temperature.

. VARIATION .

Sweet Italian Sausage Balls

Substitute ground sweet Italian sausage for spicy pork sausage, and omit jalapeño. Swap shredded Italian cheese blend for Monterey Jack cheese, parsley for cilantro, and basil for cumin. Prepare and bake as directed.

Boiled Peanuts

Makes 8 to 10 servings

These goober peas are endlessly snackable.

1 (24-ounce) package raw peanuts
½ cup kosher salt

1. In a large bowl, add peanuts and water to cover. Cover and let stand for at least 12 hours or for up to 24 hours. Drain.

2. In a large Dutch oven, bring peanuts, salt, and fresh water to cover to a boil over high heat. Reduce heat to medium, cover, and cook, stirring occasionally, until peanuts are tender, about 5 hours, adding water as necessary to keep peanuts covered. Drain before serving.

Classic Deviled Eggs,
page 62

Classic Deviled Eggs

Makes 24

"I like a lot of filling in my deviled eggs, so I mash up one whole egg with the yolks. If one of your eggs is just tearing to bits because the shell is sticking to it, that's the one to mash."—Paula

12 large eggs
½ cup mayonnaise
1 teaspoon fresh lemon juice
1 teaspoon Dijon mustard
½ teaspoon kosher salt
Toppings: relish, fresh herbs, cooked bacon, paprika

1. In a large saucepan, bring eggs and cold water to cover to a boil over medium-high heat; cook for 1 minute. Remove from heat; cover and let stand for 15 minutes. Drain eggs, and cover with ice water. Let stand until cool.

2. Peel eggs, and cut in half lengthwise. Place yolks in a medium bowl. Add mayonnaise, lemon juice, mustard, and salt to yolks; mash with a fork until well combined. Spoon yolk mixture into egg whites, and add desired toppings. Cover and refrigerate for up to 1 day.

. VARIATION .
Sour Cream and Chive Deviled Eggs

Reduce mayonnaise to ¼ cup, and add ½ cup sour cream and 2 tablespoons minced fresh chives to yolk mixture. Garnish with additional chives, if desired.

Pimiento Cheese

Makes about 5 cups

Shredding the cheese yourself is essential to achieve the right texture for the pâte of the South.
Add some chopped pickled jalapeños or a pinch of ground red pepper if you want to turn up the heat.

1½ cups mayonnaise
1 (7-ounce) jar pimientos, drained
1 tablespoon packed grated Vidalia onion, undrained
1 tablespoon Dijon mustard
2 teaspoons Worcestershire sauce
1 (16-ounce) block extra-sharp Cheddar cheese, shredded
1 (16-ounce) block extra-sharp white Cheddar cheese, shredded

1. In a large bowl, stir together mayonnaise, pimientos, onion, mustard, and Worcestershire; stir in cheeses until well combined. Cover and refrigerate for up to 1 week.

Vidalia Onion Dip

Makes about 6 cups

"God bless Vidalia, Georgia! Their famous onions are the star in this cheesy dish."—Paula

2 tablespoons butter
4 cups chopped Vidalia onions
2 cloves garlic, minced
2 (8-ounce) packages cream
 cheese, softened
1 (8-ounce) package Monterey
 Jack cheese, shredded
1 (6-ounce) package shredded
 Parmesan cheese
½ cup mayonnaise
3 tablespoons chopped fresh
 parsley
2 tablespoons Dijon mustard
1 cup chopped pecans
Garnish: chopped fresh parsley

1. Preheat oven to 350°. Spray a 1½-quart baking dish with cooking spray.
2. In a large skillet, melt butter over medium heat. Add onion and garlic; cook, stirring occasionally, until onion is tender and lightly browned, about 15 minutes.
3. In a large bowl, stir together cream cheese, cheeses, mayonnaise, parsley, and mustard until well combined; stir in onions. Spoon mixture into prepared pan, and sprinkle with pecans.
4. Bake until hot and bubbly, about 25 minutes. Garnish with parsley, if desired.

Pickled Shrimp

Makes about 12 servings

"There's a whole lot of flavor going on in this dish. The crunchy onion, sweet shrimp, and tangy marinade really perk up your taste buds and get your appetite going."—Paula

¾ cup olive oil
¾ cup apple cider vinegar
1½ teaspoons kosher salt
1½ teaspoons sugar
2 cloves garlic, minced
2 teaspoons crushed red pepper
1 teaspoon celery seeds
Hot sauce, to taste
2 pounds cooked peeled and deveined medium shrimp
1 red onion, thinly sliced
2 lemons, thinly sliced
½ cup capers, undrained
¼ cup fresh parsley leaves

1. In a large bowl, whisk together oil, vinegar, salt, sugar, garlic, red pepper, celery seeds, and hot sauce until sugar and salt are dissolved.
2. Stir in shrimp, onion, lemons, capers, and parsley until well combined. Cover and refrigerate for at least 8 hours before serving or for up to 2 days.

KITCHEN TIP

Don't refrigerate the shrimp any longer than 2 days; they will become mealy.

Marinated Crab Salad

Makes about 3 cups

You'll find variations of this dish all along the Gulf Coast. It really lets the sweet taste of fresh crab shine.

1 cup finely chopped onion, divided
1 pound lump crabmeat, picked free of shell
½ cup ice water
6 tablespoons apple cider vinegar
½ cup vegetable oil
½ teaspoon salt
¼ teaspoon ground black pepper
1 tablespoon chopped fresh parsley

1. In a small shallow dish, sprinkle ½ cup onion. Top with crabmeat and remaining ½ cup onion.

2. In a medium bowl, whisk together ½ cup ice water and vinegar; slowly whisk in oil, salt, and pepper. Pour onto crab mixture (do not stir together). Cover and refrigerate for at least 2 hours before serving or for up to 4 hours. Sprinkle with parsley just before serving.

Sweet and Sour Chicken Wings

Makes 8 to 10 servings

"These wings are a game-day favorite of all my boys, big and small."—Paula

1 cup pineapple juice
⅔ cup ketchup
2 tablespoons firmly packed light brown sugar
3 tablespoons rice vinegar
2 tablespoons soy sauce
2½ teaspoons cornstarch
¼ teaspoon garlic powder
¼ teaspoon hot sauce
2 tablespoons vegetable oil, divided
1 teaspoon salt
½ teaspoon ground black pepper
4 pounds assorted chicken wings and drumettes
2 tablespoons minced green onion

1. Preheat oven to 350°. Line a large rimmed baking sheet with foil.

2. In a large saucepan, whisk together pineapple juice, ketchup, brown sugar, vinegar, soy sauce, cornstarch, garlic powder, and hot sauce until smooth. Bring to a boil over medium-high heat, whisking constantly. Reduce heat, and simmer, whisking constantly, until thickened, about 2 minutes. Remove from heat; reserve 1 cup sauce in a small bowl for serving.

3. In a large skillet, heat 1 tablespoon oil over medium-high heat. Sprinkle salt and pepper all over chicken. Cook half of chicken until browned, about 3 minutes per side. Transfer chicken to prepared pan. Repeat procedure with remaining 1 tablespoon oil and remaining chicken. Pour remaining pineapple sauce all over chicken.

4. Bake until cooked through, about 25 minutes, turning once halfway through cooking. Let cool for 20 minutes; sprinkle with green onion, and serve with reserved pineapple sauce.

Cornmeal-Crusted Fried Pickles

Makes about 4 cups

*Try to get pickle slices that are on the thicker side; they'll hold up better
during frying and won't fall apart when you go to dip them.*

Canola oil, for frying
1½ cups plain yellow cornmeal
½ cup all-purpose flour
1 teaspoon kosher salt
1 cup whole buttermilk
4 cups garlic dill pickle slices,
 drained and patted dry
Buttermilk Ranch Sauce (recipe
 follows)

1. Fill a Dutch oven halfway with oil, and heat over medium-high
heat until a deep-fry thermometer registers 350°.

2. In a shallow dish, whisk together cornmeal, flour, and salt.
In another shallow dish, place buttermilk. Dip pickle slices in
buttermilk, letting excess drip off. Dredge in cornmeal mixture,
coating well.

3. Fry pickles in batches until golden brown, 2 to 3 minutes, adjusting
heat to maintain 350°. Let drain on paper towels; serve with
Buttermilk Ranch Sauce.

Buttermilk Ranch Sauce

Makes about 1½ cups

1 cup whole buttermilk
¼ cup mayonnaise
¼ sour cream
1 small shallot, minced
1 clove garlic, minced
1 tablespoon chopped fresh
 parsley
1 tablespoon chopped fresh dill
1 tablespoon chopped fresh
 chives
1½ teaspoons Dijon mustard
½ teaspoon salt
½ teaspoon ground black
 pepper

1. In a small bowl, whisk together all ingredients. Cover and
refrigerate for up to 3 days.

Spicy–Sweet Mixed Nuts

Makes about 4 cups

*These crunchy nuts are great to have on hand for snacking,
and they also make nice gifts during the holidays.*

1 egg white
2 tablespoons firmly packed
  light brown sugar
1 teaspoon salt
1 teaspoon chili powder
½ teaspoon ground coriander
¼ teaspoon ground red pepper
1 cup pecan halves
1 cup whole cashews
1 cup whole almonds
1 cup unsalted peanuts

1. Preheat oven to 325°. Line a large rimmed baking sheet with parchment paper.

2. In a large bowl, whisk egg white until foamy; whisk in brown sugar, salt, chili powder, coriander, and red pepper until well combined. Stir in nuts until well coated. Spread in a single layer on prepared pan.

3. Bake for 15 minutes. Stir and bake 5 minutes more. Let cool completely. Store in an airtight container for up to 1 week.

Sausage Cheese Dip

Makes 8 to 10 servings

"This is always the first snack to go at any potluck I make it for. You can stir it together a day ahead and refrigerate it until you're ready to bake it."—Paula

1 pound ground pork sausage
1 cup chopped onion
2 (8-ounce) packages cream cheese, softened
1 (8-ounce) package shredded mozzarella cheese
1 (6-ounce) package shredded Parmesan cheese
½ cup sour cream
½ cup mayonnaise
½ cup minced roasted red peppers

1. Preheat oven to 350°. Spray a 1½-quart baking dish with cooking spray.

2. In a large skillet, cook sausage and onion over medium heat, stirring frequently, until sausage is browned and crumbly; drain well.

3. In a large bowl, stir together cream cheese, cheeses, sour cream, and mayonnaise until well combined. Stir in sausage mixture and peppers. Spoon mixture into prepared pan.

4. Bake until hot and bubbly, about 30 minutes. Let stand for 5 minutes before serving.

Classic Pairings

SOUPS, SALADS, AND SANDWICHES

Soups are the original one-dish meal, and they still reign supreme. It's so easy for me to throw a batch of ingredients together and let them simmer away while I tend to other things. And of course, salads and sandwiches are the ultimate soup pairings for creating easy lunches and dinners. I know you'll enjoy serving up hearty, warming meals with these versatile recipes.

Chicken and Biscuit Dumplings

Makes about 8 servings

Warm, comforting chicken and dumplings are about as Southern as it gets.

Chicken broth:

- 1 (4½-pound) whole chicken
- 4 stalks celery, cut into 3-inch pieces
- 4 medium carrots, peeled and cut into 3-inch pieces
- 1 medium onion, peeled and cut into wedges
- 1 tablespoon black peppercorns

Stew:

- 3 tablespoons unsalted butter
- 1½ cups chopped onion
- 1½ cups chopped carrot
- 1 cup chopped celery
- 2 cloves garlic, minced
- ⅓ cup all-purpose flour
- ½ cup heavy whipping cream
- 1 tablespoon chopped fresh thyme
- 1 tablespoon chopped fresh sage
- 1 tablespoon chopped fresh parsley
- 2¼ teaspoons kosher salt
- ½ teaspoon ground black pepper

Dumplings:

- 1½ cups all-purpose flour
- 1 teaspoon baking powder
- ¾ teaspoon kosher salt
- ⅛ teaspoon ground black pepper
- ½ cup whole buttermilk
- 1 tablespoon unsalted butter, melted
- 1 large egg

Garnish: chopped fresh parsley

1. For chicken broth: In a large Dutch oven, bring chicken, celery, carrot, onion, peppercorns, and water to cover by 1 inch to a boil over medium-high heat. Reduce heat to medium, and simmer until chicken is tender, about 2 hours.

2. Remove chicken from broth, and let cool enough to handle. Shred meat, discarding skin and bones. Strain broth through a fine-mesh sieve, discarding solids. Reserve 4 cups broth for stew; freeze remaining broth for another use.

3. For stew: In a large Dutch oven, melt butter over medium-high heat. Add onion, carrot, and celery; cook until just soft, about 3 minutes. Stir in garlic; cook for 1 minute. Stir in 2 cups reserved broth, and bring to a boil. Reduce heat, cover, and simmer until vegetables are crisp-tender, about 7 minutes.

4. In a small bowl, whisk together flour and remaining 2 cups reserved broth; stir into vegetables. Stir in cream, thyme, sage, parsley, salt, and pepper. Cook over medium heat, stirring frequently, until mixture thickens, about 8 minutes. Remove from heat; stir in shredded chicken.

5. For dumplings: In a medium bowl, whisk together flour, baking powder, salt, and pepper. Make a well in center of dry ingredients. In a small bowl, whisk together buttermilk, melted butter, and egg; stir buttermilk mixture into flour mixture until a dough forms. Using floured hands, roll dough into 1-inch balls.

6. Bring stew to a boil over medium-high heat. Quickly drop dough balls into stew (do not stir). Cover, reduce heat, and simmer (do not continue to boil) without stirring, until dumplings are puffed and cooked through, about 15 minutes. Garnish with parsley, if desired.

Smoked Boston Butt Sandwiches

Makes 10 to 12 servings

This makes a huge amount of meat for sandwiches—you can definitely feed a crowd.

Mesquite wood chips, soaked in
   water for 30 minutes
3 tablespoons firmly packed
   light brown sugar
2 tablespoons chili powder
2 teaspoons salt
1 teaspoon garlic powder
1 teaspoon onion powder
1 teaspoon ground black
   pepper
1 (7-pound) Boston butt pork
   roast
Sandwich bread
Classic Barbecue Sauce (recipe
   follows)

1. Prepare smoker according to manufacturer's directions for an internal temperature to 225° to 250°; maintain temperature for 15 to 20 minutes. Sprinkle soaked wood chips onto coals.

2. In a small bowl, stir together brown sugar, chili powder, salt, garlic powder, onion powder, and pepper; rub mixture all over roast. Place roast, fat side up, on upper rack in smoker, and place a drip pan under rack.

3. Cover smoker with lid; smoke roast, maintaining temperature inside smoker between 225° and 250°, until a meat thermometer inserted in thickest portion registers 190°, 9 to 11 hours. Remove roast from heat, and let stand for 30 minutes. Shred roast, discarding fat and bone. Serve on bread with Classic Barbecue Sauce.

Classic Barbecue Sauce

Makes 3 cups

2 cups ketchup
1½ cups firmly packed light
   brown sugar
½ cup red wine vinegar
2 tablespoons dry mustard
1 tablespoon Worcestershire
   sauce
1 tablespoon hot sauce
2 teaspoons onion powder
2 teaspoons salt
2 teaspoons paprika
1½ teaspoons ground black
   pepper

1. In a medium saucepan, whisk together all ingredients; bring to a boil over medium-high heat. Reduce heat, and simmer, whisking frequently, for 10 minutes. Let cool completely. Refrigerate in an airtight container for up to 2 weeks.

Fried Shrimp Po' Boys

Makes 4 servings

*"I can never get enough shrimp. Living on the Georgia coast has made me spoiled,
and I think po' boys are a great way to enjoy fresh seafood."—Paula*

½ cup whole milk
2 large eggs
1 cup all-purpose flour
½ cup plain yellow cornmeal
1 teaspoon Cajun seasoning
Vegetable oil, for frying
1½ pounds large fresh shrimp,
    peeled and deveined
Shredded lettuce
Sliced tomatoes
4 hoagie or sub rolls, split
    lengthwise
Spicy Lemon Cream Sauce (recipe
    follows)

1. In a medium bowl, whisk together milk and eggs. In another medium bowl, whisk together flour, cornmeal, and Cajun seasoning.

2. In a large Dutch oven, pour oil to a depth of 2 inches, and heat over medium heat until a deep-fry thermometer registers 350°. Dredge shrimp in milk mixture, letting excess drip off. Dredge in flour mixture to fully coat.

3. Fry shrimp in batches until golden brown, about 3 minutes. Let drain on paper towels. Layer lettuce, tomato, and shrimp in rolls, and top with Spicy Lemon Cream Sauce. Serve immediately.

Spicy Lemon Cream Sauce

Makes about 1½ cups

1 cup mayonnaise
¼ cup Sriracha sauce
1 tablespoon fresh lemon juice
1 tablespoon soy sauce

1. In a small bowl, whisk together all ingredients. Cover and refrigerate for up to 3 days.

New Year's Day Soup

Makes about 5 quarts

This soup brings together pork, greens, and black-eyed peas for good luck in the New Year or whenever you decide to make it. It's good all year long!

2 tablespoons extra-virgin olive oil

2 cups chopped sweet onion

1 tablespoon chopped fresh garlic

3 (32-ounce) cartons low-sodium chicken broth

1 (28-ounce) can diced tomatoes

3 (15.8-ounce) cans black-eyed peas, drained

2 pounds country ham, cubed

1 (16-ounce) package chopped fresh turnip greens

3 tablespoons apple cider vinegar

1 tablespoon seasoned salt

1. In a large Dutch oven, heat oil over medium-high heat. Add onion and garlic; cook, stirring frequently, until translucent, about 2 minutes. Stir in broth and tomatoes, and bring to a boil. Stir in peas, ham, greens, vinegar, and seasoned salt until greens are wilted, and bring to a boil. Reduce heat to medium-low, and cook for 15 minutes. Serve immediately.

—————————— **KITCHEN TIP** ——————————

Swap collard or mustard greens for turnip greens if you prefer.

Fruit Salad with Sweet Orange Dressing

Makes 6 to 8 servings

This salad tastes as good as it looks.

Bibb lettuce leaves
1 **Granny Smith apple,
   quartered and thinly sliced**
1 **English cucumber, thinly
   sliced**
2 **navel oranges, peeled and
   sliced**
1 **cup fresh blueberries**
1 **cup halved fresh strawberries**
Sweet Orange Dressing (recipe
   follows)
Garnish: fresh mint

1. On a serving platter, arrange lettuce, apple, cucumber, oranges, blueberries, and strawberries. Drizzle with Sweet Orange Dressing just before serving. Garnish with mint, if desired.

Sweet Orange Dressing

Makes about 1 cup

¼ **cup water**
¼ **cup sugar**
2 **sprigs fresh mint**
3 **tablespoons rice vinegar**
1 **tablespoon orange zest**
¼ **teaspoon kosher salt**
3 **tablespoons olive oil**
2 **tablespoons chopped fresh
   basil**

1. In a small saucepan, cook ¼ cup water and sugar over medium-high heat, stirring frequently, until sugar is dissolved. Remove from heat, and add mint sprigs. Cover and let stand for 30 minutes; discard mint.
2. In a medium bowl, whisk together mint syrup, vinegar, zest, and salt; whisk in oil and basil. Cover and refrigerate for up to 3 days.

Paula's Chicken
Salad Sandwiches,
page 89

Paula's Chicken Salad Sandwiches

Makes about 5 cups

"I always have some chicken salad on hand in my fridge. It's a great snack to have anytime."—Paula

½ cup mayonnaise
2 tablespoons fresh lemon juice
1 teaspoon salt
3½ cups chopped cooked chicken
1 cup diced celery
⅓ cup slivered almonds
Sandwich bread
Green leaf lettuce
Sliced tomato

1. In a medium bowl, stir together mayonnaise, lemon juice, and salt. Stir in chicken, celery, and almonds until well combined. Cover and refrigerate for up to 3 days. Serve on bread with lettuce and tomato.

KITCHEN TIP

Pick up a rotisserie chicken from the deli section
of your grocery store to make this recipe in a flash.

Chicken Corn Chowder

Makes 8 to 10 servings

A few items from the freezer section of the grocery store make this soup an easy weeknight meal.

4 tablespoons butter, divided

1¾ pounds boneless skinless chicken breasts, cut into ½-inch pieces

½ teaspoon salt

½ teaspoon ground black pepper

1 cup minced red bell pepper

½ cup minced green onion

3 cups frozen diced hash brown potatoes, thawed

1 (10-ounce) package frozen whole kernel corn, thawed

¼ cup all-purpose flour

6 cups chicken broth

1 cup sour cream

Garnish: sliced green onion

1. In a Dutch oven, melt 2 tablespoons butter over medium-high heat. Sprinkle chicken with salt and pepper; cook, stirring occasionally, for 5 minutes. Transfer chicken to a plate.

2. Melt remaining 2 tablespoons butter in pot over medium heat. Add bell pepper and green onion; cook for 2 minutes. Stir in hash browns and corn; cook, stirring frequently, until potatoes are just tender, 6 to 8 minutes. Stir in flour; cook, stirring constantly, for 2 minutes. Stir in broth.

3. Return chicken to pot, and bring to a boil over medium heat. Reduce heat, and simmer, stirring occasionally, until mixture is thickened, 15 to 20 minutes. Remove from heat, and stir in sour cream. Garnish with green onion, if desired.

7-Layer Salad

Makes 10 to 12 servings

This is a great summertime make-ahead, no-cook dish.

6 cups chopped romaine lettuce
4 cups seeded chopped tomato
4 cups seeded chopped cucumber
1 (16-ounce) package frozen baby peas, thawed and drained
½ cup sliced green onion
2 cups sliced radishes
2 cups sour cream
1 cup mayonnaise
¼ cup fresh lemon juice
2 teaspoons salt
1½ cups shredded sharp Cheddar cheese
6 slices bacon, chopped and cooked

1. In a large trifle dish or serving bowl, layer lettuce, tomato, and cucumber.

2. In a medium bowl, stir together peas and green onion; spread onto cucumber, and top with radishes.

3. In same bowl, stir together sour cream, mayonnaise, lemon juice, and salt. Spread onto radishes, sealing edges. Top with cheese and bacon. Cover tightly with plastic wrap, and refrigerate for at least 8 hours before serving or for up to 24 hours. Let stand at room temperature for 15 minutes before serving.

Seared Snapper, Corn, and Onion Salad

Makes 2 servings

*This simple salad is a great way to use your fresh farmers' market
produce, and the addition of fish makes it a full meal.*

1 tablespoon chili powder
1 tablespoon ground cumin
1 teaspoon salt
1 teaspoon garlic powder
½ teaspoon ground black
    pepper
1 small onion, cut into
    ½-inch-thick rings
¾ cup fresh corn kernels
2 skinless red snapper fillets
2 tablespoons olive oil, divided
6 cups torn romaine lettuce
¾ cup chopped tomato
Creamy Lime Cumin Dressing
    (recipe follows)

1. In a small bowl, whisk together chili powder, cumin, salt, garlic powder, and pepper; sprinkle onto onion, corn, and fish.
2. In a large skillet, heat 1 tablespoon oil over medium-high heat. Add onion; cook for 2 minutes. Add corn; cook for 1 minute. Remove from skillet.
3. Add remaining 1 tablespoon oil to skillet. Add fish; cook until fish flakes easily with a fork, about 3 minutes per side. Break into 1-inch pieces.
4. Divide lettuce, tomato, onion, corn, and fish between 2 plates; serve immediately with Creamy Lime Cumin Dressing.

Creamy Lime Cumin Dressing

Makes about 1½ cups

1 cup sour cream
½ cup whole milk
1 teaspoon lime zest
1 tablespoon fresh lime juice
¼ teaspoon salt
¼ teaspoon ground cumin
⅛ teaspoon chili powder
⅛ teaspoon sugar

1. In a small bowl, whisk together all ingredients. Cover and refrigerate for at least 2 hours before serving or for up to 3 days.

Chicken, Sausage, and Okra Gumbo

Makes 10 to 12 servings

*Every good gumbo starts with the trinity, the blend of onion, bell pepper,
and celery that forms the base of many savory Cajun and Creole dishes.*

¾ cup plus 2 tablespoons
   vegetable oil, divided
2 pounds boneless skinless
   chicken thighs, cut into bite-
   size pieces
¾ pound smoked andouille
   sausage, sliced ¼ inch thick
1 cup all-purpose flour
2 cups chopped onion
1 cup chopped celery
1 cup chopped green bell
   pepper
2 cloves garlic, minced
2 (32-ounce) cartons chicken
   broth
1 (15-ounce) package frozen
   chopped okra
2 bay leaves
1 tablespoon Worcestershire
   sauce
1 teaspoon hot sauce
¾ teaspoon dried thyme
½ teaspoon ground black
   pepper
Hot cooked rice
Garnish: chopped green onion

1. In a large Dutch oven, heat 2 tablespoons oil over medium heat. Cook chicken and sausage in batches, stirring frequently, until browned on all sides, about 10 minutes. Remove from pot, and let drain on paper towels.

2. Add remaining ¾ cup oil to pot, and heat over medium-low heat. Whisk in flour until smooth; cook, whisking frequently, until mixture is chocolate colored, 30 to 40 minutes.

3. Stir in onion, celery, bell pepper, and garlic; cook, stirring occasionally, until vegetables are just tender, about 15 minutes. Gradually stir in broth until well combined. Stir in chicken, sausage, okra, bay leaves, Worcestershire, hot sauce, thyme, and pepper, and bring to a boil. Reduce heat, and simmer, uncovered, stirring occasionally, for 2½ to 3 hours.

4. Discard bay leaves. Serve with rice. Garnish with green onion, if desired.

─────────────── **KITCHEN TIP** ───────────────

Swap frozen okra for 2 cups sliced fresh okra when it's in season.

Caramelized Onion Patty Melts

Makes 6

The Tangy Sauce adds major flavor to this diner standard and any other sandwich, burger, or hot dog you put it on.

8 tablespoons unsalted butter, divided
3 medium Vidalia onions, thinly sliced
1½ pounds ground beef
2 teaspoons Worcestershire sauce
1 teaspoon kosher salt
½ teaspoon ground black pepper
12 slices sourdough bread
Tangy Sauce (recipe follows)
6 slices Cheddar cheese

1. In a large cast-iron skillet, melt 2 tablespoons butter over medium heat. Add onion; cook, stirring occasionally, until soft and golden brown, about 35 minutes. Transfer to a medium bowl; wipe skillet clean with a paper towel.

2. In a large bowl, stir together beef, Worcestershire, salt, and pepper. Divide mixture into 6 portions, and shape each into a patty.

3. Cook patties in skillet over medium-high heat until browned and cooked through, about 3 minutes per side. Remove patties from skillet; wipe skillet clean with a paper towel.

4. Layer half of bread slices with Tangy Sauce, onions, 1 slice cheese, patty, more Tangy Sauce, and bread.

5. Melt 2 tablespoons butter in skillet over medium-high heat. Cook 2 sandwiches until golden brown and cheese is melted, about 3 minutes per side. Repeat with remaining 4 tablespoons butter and sandwiches. Serve immediately.

Tangy Sauce

Makes about ½ cup

¼ cup mayonnaise
¼ cup Dijon mustard
1 tablespoon barbecue sauce
½ teaspoon hot sauce

1. In a small bowl, whisk together all ingredients. Cover and refrigerate for up to 3 days.

Muffuletta

Makes 12 servings

"When you're in New Orleans, you have to get a muffuletta from Central Grocery. One time I was there, I looked up and, lo and behold, actor John Goodman was in line ahead of me ordering a sandwich. I knew then and there I was in the right place."—Paula

1 (12-ounce) jar marinated artichoke hearts, drained and chopped
½ cup giardiniera, chopped
½ cup green olives, chopped
½ cup Kalamata olives, chopped
½ cup shredded carrot
¼ cup shredded celery
¼ cup capers, drained and chopped
¼ cup chopped pepperoncini peppers
2 tablespoons red wine vinegar
2 teaspoons dried oregano
2 (1-pound) loaves ciabatta bread, halved horizontally
1 pound thinly sliced Genoa salami
1 pound thinly sliced ham
1 pound thinly sliced mortadella
1 pound thinly sliced mozzarella
1 pound thinly sliced provolone
1 bunch fresh basil leaves

1. In a medium bowl, stir together artichokes, giardiniera, all olives, carrot, celery, capers, pepperoncini, vinegar, and oregano.

2. Remove center of bread in bottom half of loaves; spread artichoke mixture onto bottom halves, and layer each with half of meats, cheeses, and basil. Cover with top half of loaves, and wrap each tightly in plastic wrap. Refrigerate for at least 3 hours before serving or up to overnight; cut each sandwich into 6 slices to serve.

KITCHEN TIP

Giardiniera is a blend of pickled vegetables, typically containing cauliflower, carrots, bell peppers, celery, and onion. You'll find it with the pickles and relish in grocery stores.

Down South Burgers

Makes 6

"These are my ultimate burgers for a summer cookout."—Paula

2 pounds ground chuck
2 tablespoons Worcestershire
   sauce
1 teaspoon garlic salt
½ teaspoon ground black
   pepper
1½ cups shredded Gruyère
   cheese
6 hamburger buns, halved
Rémoulade Sauce (recipe follows)
Green leaf lettuce
6 Fried Green Tomatoes (recipe
   on page 125)
1 small red onion, thinly sliced

1. Spray grill with nonflammable cooking spray. Preheat grill to medium-high heat (350° to 400°).

2. In a large bowl, stir together beef, Worcestershire, garlic salt, and pepper. Divide mixture into 6 portions, and shape each into a patty.

3. Grill patties, covered with grill lid, to desired doneness, 4 to 5 minutes per side. Top each patty with ¼ cup cheese. Cook, covered with grill lid, until cheese is melted, about 1 minute. Grill buns, cut side down, until toasted, 1 to 2 minutes.

4. Spread Rémoulade Sauce onto bottom half of buns; top with lettuce, Fried Green Tomatoes, patties, onion, more rémoulade, and bun tops. Serve immediately.

Rémoulade Sauce

Makes about 2 cups

1 cup mayonnaise
3 tablespoons ketchup
2 tablespoons minced green
   onion
2 tablespoons minced celery
1 tablespoon minced fresh
   parsley
1 tablespoon fresh lemon juice
1 tablespoon sweet pickle
   relish
1 tablespoon whole-grain
   mustard
2 teaspoons Creole seasoning

1. In a small bowl, whisk together all ingredients. Cover and refrigerate for up to 5 days.

Grilled Grouper Sandwiches

Makes 6

Grouper is a good choice for sandwiches because it has a nice, meaty texture.
Any firm white fish such as catfish, cod, or halibut can be used in its place.

6 (4-ounce) grouper fillets
¼ cup olive oil
1½ teaspoons kosher salt
1½ teaspoons ground black
   pepper
6 hamburger buns, halved
1 (5-ounce) bag fresh baby
   spinach
12 thin tomato slices
Homemade Spicy Mayonnaise
   (recipe follows)

1. Heat a grill pan over medium-high heat.
2. Brush both sides of fish fillets with oil; sprinkle with salt and pepper. Cook until fish is cooked through, 5 to 7 minutes per side. Cook buns, cut side down, until toasted, about 2 minutes.
3. Top bottom half of buns with spinach, tomato, fish, Homemade Spicy Mayonnaise, and bun tops. Serve immediately.

Homemade Spicy Mayonnaise

Makes about 1 cup

2 chipotle peppers in adobo
   sauce
2 cloves garlic, minced
3 tablespoons fresh lime juice
2 large pasteurized egg yolks
½ teaspoon kosher salt
½ cup extra-virgin olive oil
½ cup avocado oil

1. In the work bowl of a food processor, pulse together chipotles in adobo, garlic, lime juice, egg yolks, and salt until well combined. With processor running, add oils in a slow, steady stream until mixture is thick and smooth. Cover and refrigerate for up to 3 days.

Creamy Coleslaw

Makes 8 to 10 servings

Never go empty-handed to a potluck again with this mix-and-stir slaw.

½ cup Durkee Famous Sandwich & Salad Sauce
3 tablespoons white wine vinegar
2 tablespoons mayonnaise
½ teaspoon celery salt
½ teaspoon seasoned pepper
1 (10-ounce) package angel hair coleslaw
½ (10-ounce) package matchstick carrots
¾ cup diced seeded cucumber

1. In a large bowl, whisk together Durkee Sauce, vinegar, mayonnaise, celery salt, and pepper. Stir in slaw, carrots, and cucumber until well combined. Refrigerate, stirring occasionally, for at least 1 hour before serving or for up to 2 days.

Classic Potato Salad

Makes 8 to 10 servings

Red potatoes add good color to this comforting side dish.

1 (3-pound) bag small red potatoes, quartered
½ cup mayonnaise
½ cup sour cream
1 teaspoon salt
1 teaspoon ground black pepper
10 slices bacon, chopped and cooked
5 large hard-cooked eggs, peeled and chopped
1 cup chopped celery
¼ cup minced red onion
1 tablespoon minced fresh dill

1. In a large Dutch oven, bring potatoes and cold water to cover to a boil over medium-high heat. Reduce heat, and simmer until tender, about 8 minutes. Drain well.
2. In a large bowl, stir together mayonnaise, sour cream, salt, and pepper. Stir in potatoes and all remaining ingredients until well combined. Cover and refrigerate for at least 1 hour before serving or for up to 3 days.

Southern Sides

VEGETABLES AND MORE

It's sometimes a toss-up for me to pick my favorite vegetables. When I slice a nice and juicy, ripe tomato for a sandwich on white bread, I think that's the ultimate Southern veggie, but when okra's in season and I pop a few fried nuggets in my mouth, I rethink it all. And sweet potatoes can't be beat in the fall, until the collards and turnips start coming in. In my book, just about the best produce you can eat comes from a Southern garden, and these recipes celebrate it all.

Summer Squash Casserole

Makes 6 to 8 servings

"Make your way through a bumper crop of squash and zucchini with this creamy, cheesy casserole."—Paula

2 pounds yellow squash, sliced
2 pounds zucchini, sliced
¾ cup butter, divided
1½ cups diced onion
2 teaspoons minced garlic
½ cup sour cream
½ cup mayonnaise
2 large eggs
2 cups shredded white Cheddar cheese
2 cups shredded extra-sharp Cheddar cheese
1 cup shredded fontina cheese
1 cup panko (Japanese bread crumbs)
2 teaspoons kosher salt
2 teaspoons ground black pepper
2½ cups crushed buttery round crackers

1. Preheat oven to 350°. Spray a 13x9-inch baking dish with cooking spray.

2. In a Dutch oven, bring squash, zucchini, and water to cover to a boil over high heat. Cook until just tender, about 5 minutes. Drain well.

3. In a medium skillet, melt ¼ cup butter over medium-high heat. Add onion and garlic; cook, stirring frequently, until tender, about 10 minutes.

4. In a large bowl, whisk together sour cream, mayonnaise, and eggs. Stir in squash mixture, onion mixture, cheeses, bread crumbs, salt, and pepper. Pour into prepared pan.

5. In a medium microwave-safe bowl, melt remaining ½ cup butter; stir in cracker crumbs until well combined. Sprinkle onto casserole, and cover with foil.

6. Bake for 20 minutes. Uncover and bake until golden brown, 25 to 30 minutes more. Let stand for 10 minutes before serving.

--- **KITCHEN TIP** ---

The casserole can be prepared through step 4, covered, and refrigerated overnight.
Let it stand at room temperature for 30 minutes before proceeding with recipe.

Old-Fashioned Green Beans

Makes 6 to 8 servings

"Bacon makes everything better. Try these green beans, and you'll know what I mean."—Paula

5 slices bacon, chopped
2 pounds fresh green beans, trimmed and halved crosswise
1 (16-ounce) package frozen pearl onions, thawed
1 (32-ounce) carton chicken broth
½ teaspoon ground black pepper

1. In a large Dutch oven, cook bacon over medium heat until crisp. Add green beans and onions; cook, stirring occasionally, for 5 minutes.
2. Stir in broth and pepper, and bring to a boil over high heat. Reduce heat, cover, and simmer until beans and onion are tender, about 30 minutes.

Creamed Corn

Makes 4 to 6 servings

*To make this iconic Southern dish year-round, use two 16-ounce packages
of frozen corn kernels when fresh isn't available.*

6 slices bacon, chopped
4 cups fresh corn kernels
(about 6 large ears corn)
½ cup chopped onion
1 tablespoon all-purpose flour
1½ cups heavy whipping cream
1½ teaspoons sugar
½ teaspoon salt
½ teaspoon ground black
pepper

1. In a large skillet, cook bacon over medium heat until crisp. Remove bacon using a slotted spoon, and let drain on paper towels, reserving drippings in skillet.

2. Add corn and onion to drippings; cook, stirring occasionally, for 10 minutes. Stir in flour; cook, stirring constantly, for 2 minutes. Stir in cream, sugar, salt, and pepper; cook, stirring frequently, until thickened, about 15 minutes. Top with bacon just before serving.

Herbed Bacon and Hash Brown Casserole

Makes 8 to 10 servings

This is a terrific side dish for grilled chicken, pork chops, ham, or turkey.

1 (16-ounce) package bacon, chopped

¼ cup butter

1 green bell pepper, chopped

1 onion, chopped

1 tablespoon minced garlic

2 cups sour cream

1 (10.5-ounce) can cream of chicken soup

1 (10.5-ounce) can cream of mushroom soup

2 (32-ounce) packages frozen hash brown potatoes, thawed

1 (8-ounce) package sharp Cheddar cheese, shredded

3 tablespoons chopped fresh parsley, divided

2 tablespoons chopped fresh dill

1 teaspoon minced fresh thyme

1 teaspoon salt

1 cup shredded Gouda cheese

1 cup panko (Japanese bread crumbs)

1. Preheat oven to 350°. Spray a 3-quart baking dish with cooking spray.

2. In a large skillet, cook bacon over medium heat until crisp. Remove bacon using a slotted spoon, and let drain on paper towels. Pour off drippings, and wipe skillet clean.

3. In same skillet, melt butter over medium heat. Add bell pepper, onion, and garlic; cook, stirring occasionally, until tender, about 8 minutes.

4. In a large bowl, whisk together sour cream and soups; stir in cooked vegetables, hash browns, Cheddar, 2 tablespoons parsley, dill, thyme, salt, and two-thirds of cooked bacon. Spoon mixture into prepared pan, and cover with foil.

5. Bake for 45 minutes.

6. In a small bowl, stir together Gouda, bread crumbs, remaining 1 tablespoon parsley, and remaining bacon. Uncover casserole, and sprinkle with Gouda mixture. Bake until hot and bubbly and topping is golden brown, about 30 minutes more. Let stand for 10 minutes before serving.

Summer Succotash

Makes 8 to 10 servings

The gifts of a Southern garden beautifully come together in this classic side dish.

3 cups fresh baby lima beans
2 cups fresh lady peas
¼ cup butter
2 tablespoons olive oil
¾ cup chopped green onion
1 tablespoon minced garlic
4 cups fresh corn kernels
   (about 6 large ears corn)
2 cups heavy whipping cream
2 tablespoons chopped fresh
   thyme
1½ teaspoons salt
1 teaspoon sugar
1 teaspoon garlic powder
½ teaspoon ground black pepper
1 pint grape tomatoes,
   quartered

1. In a medium saucepan, bring beans, peas, and water to cover to a boil over medium-high heat. Reduce heat, and cook until tender, 10 to 15 minutes. Drain well.

2. In a large skillet, melt butter with oil over medium heat. Add green onion and garlic; cook, stirring frequently, for 3 minutes.

3. Stir in beans, peas, corn, cream, thyme, salt, sugar, garlic powder, and pepper; cook, stirring occasionally, for 20 minutes. Stir in tomatoes, and cook until heated through, about 2 minutes. Serve immediately.

Broccoli, Rice, and Cheese Casserole

Makes 8 to 10 servings

This easy side dish is a potluck staple.

4 heads fresh broccoli, cut into
   florets
¾ cup chopped onion
4 cloves garlic, minced
1 tablespoon salt
1 (10.75-ounce) can cream of
   mushroom soup
1 cup sour cream
1 large egg
2 cups cooked long-grain rice
3 cups shredded Cheddar
   cheese, divided
2½ cups crushed saltine crackers,
   divided
¼ cup butter, melted

1. Preheat oven to 350°. Spray a 13x9-inch baking dish with cooking spray.

2. In a large saucepan, bring broccoli, onion, garlic, salt, and water to cover to a boil over high heat. Reduce heat, and simmer until broccoli is crisp-tender, about 5 minutes. Drain well, and let cool.

3. In a large bowl, whisk together soup, sour cream, and egg. Stir in broccoli mixture, rice, 2 cups cheese, and 1 cup crushed crackers. Pour into prepared pan.

4. In a medium bowl, stir together melted butter, remaining 1½ cups crackers, and remaining 1 cup cheese. Sprinkle onto casserole.

5. Bake until hot and bubbly, about 30 minutes. Let stand for 5 minutes before serving.

Marinated Vegetable
Salad, page 119

Marinated Vegetable Salad

Makes 2 quarts

*This is a great salad for a cookout because it contains no dairy
and can sit out awhile without worry of spoiling.*

2 cups white wine vinegar
1 cup rice vinegar
¼ cup sugar
2 tablespoons kosher salt
2 teaspoons mustard seeds
3 large cucumbers, scored and sliced about ¼ inch thick
1½ large Vidalia or other sweet onions, thinly sliced
6 dried red chiles
1 pint cherry or grape tomatoes, halved
2 medium tomatoes, quartered
1 teaspoon ground black pepper

1. In a large bowl, whisk together vinegars, sugar, salt, and mustard seeds until sugar and salt are dissolved.

2. Stir in cucumber, onion, and chiles until well combined. Cover and refrigerate overnight.

3. Just before serving, stir in tomatoes and pepper. Serve with a slotted spoon.

KITCHEN TIP

It's easy to cut a bunch of cherry tomatoes in half at one time by placing them between two plastic lids and cutting through them horizontally all in one stroke. Lids from take-out containers work great; place the bottom lid rim side up and the top lid rim side down. The grooves on the lids help hold the tomatoes in place as you slice through them. This works with pitted olives, too.

Caramelized Vidalia Onion Tart

Makes 1 (10-inch) tart

Cheese, cheese, and more cheese makes this onion tart a decadent side for any meal.

½ (14.1-ounce) package refrigerated piecrusts
¼ cup butter
5 large Vidalia onions, thinly sliced
2 tablespoons balsamic vinegar
1 (8-ounce) package cream cheese, softened
1 (4-ounce) package goat cheese, softened
1½ cups shredded Gruyère cheese, divided
2 egg yolks, lightly beaten
1 tablespoon minced fresh thyme
¼ teaspoon salt
¼ teaspoon ground black pepper

1. Preheat oven to 425°.

2. On a lightly floured surface, roll dough to a 12-inch circle. Press into bottom and up sides of a 10-inch removable-bottom tart pan. Prick all over with a fork.

3. Bake for 6 minutes. Let cool completely. Reduce oven temperature to 350°.

4. In a large skillet, melt butter over medium heat. Add onion; cover and cook, stirring occasionally, until tender, about 20 minutes. Uncover and increase heat to medium-high. Cook, stirring frequently, until onion is lightly browned, 10 to 15 minutes. Stir in vinegar, and cook for 2 minutes.

5. Remove from heat, and stir in cream cheese, goat cheese, and 1 cup Gruyère until melted and smooth. Stir in egg yolks, thyme, salt, and pepper. Spread mixture into prepared crust.

6. Bake for 25 minutes. Sprinkle with remaining ½ cup Gruyère, and bake 5 minutes more. Let cool on a wire rack for 15 minutes. Remove from pan, and serve warm.

Cheesy Bacon Sweet Potato Casserole

Makes 6 to 8 servings

*Rosemary and thyme make this sweet potato casserole a wonderful flavor change
from the expected marshmallow-topped version.*

6 slices bacon, chopped
1 large yellow onion, thinly
sliced
1 teaspoon chopped fresh
thyme
1 teaspoon chopped fresh
rosemary
6 cups mashed cooked sweet
potato
1½ cups shredded Gruyère
cheese, divided
½ cup heavy whipping cream
¼ cup unsalted butter, melted
1 large egg, lightly beaten
1½ teaspoons kosher salt
¼ teaspoon ground black pepper
Garnish: chopped fresh rosemary

1. Preheat oven to 350°. Spray a 2-quart baking dish with cooking spray.

2. In a large skillet, cook bacon over medium heat until crisp. Remove bacon using a slotted spoon, and let drain on paper towels, reserving drippings in skillet. Add onion to drippings; cook, stirring frequently, until golden brown, about 30 minutes. Stir in thyme and rosemary, and remove from heat.

3. In a large bowl, stir together onion mixture, sweet potato, 1 cup cheese, cream, melted butter, egg, salt, and pepper. Spoon mixture into prepared pan.

4. Bake until heated through, about 30 minutes. Top with remaining ½ cup cheese, and bake until melted, about 5 minutes more. Top with bacon just before serving; garnish with rosemary, if desired.

Heirloom Tomato Pie

Makes 1 (10-inch) pie

Cradled in a buttery cornmeal crust, this Southern staple sings with flavor and bright color.

1⅔ cups all-purpose flour

⅓ cup plus 1 tablespoon plain cornmeal, divided

3½ teaspoons kosher salt, divided

¾ cup cold unsalted butter, cubed

6 to 8 tablespoons cold whole buttermilk

8 medium assorted heirloom tomatoes, sliced ¼ inch thick (about 3 pounds)

½ cup halved assorted small heirloom tomatoes

¾ cup shredded sharp white Cheddar cheese, divided

⅔ cup mayonnaise

1 tablespoon chopped fresh thyme

1 tablespoon chopped fresh parsley

1 tablespoon chopped fresh oregano

¼ teaspoon ground black pepper

2 teaspoons red wine vinegar

Garnish: chopped fresh basil

1. In the work bowl of a food processor, pulse together flour, ⅓ cup cornmeal, and 1½ teaspoons salt. Add cold butter, pulsing until mixture is crumbly. Gradually add buttermilk, pulsing until a dough forms.

2. Turn out dough onto a lightly floured surface, and shape into a disk. Wrap tightly in plastic wrap, and refrigerate for at least 30 minutes.

3. Line a baking sheet with paper towels. Place tomatoes on paper towels; sprinkle with remaining 2 teaspoons salt. Let stand for 30 minutes. Pat dry with paper towels.

4. Preheat oven to 425°. Sprinkle remaining 1 tablespoon cornmeal in a 10-inch cast-iron skillet.

5. On a lightly floured surface, roll dough to a 13-inch circle. Press into bottom and up sides of prepared skillet, letting excess extend over sides of skillet.

6. In a small bowl, stir together ½ cup cheese, mayonnaise, thyme, parsley, oregano, and pepper. Spread onto dough. Layer tomato slices onto filling; top with halved tomatoes, and drizzle with vinegar. Fold excess dough over tomatoes at edges.

7. Bake until crust is golden brown, about 30 minutes. Sprinkle with remaining ¼ cup cheese; bake until melted, about 5 minutes more. Let cool on a wire rack for 30 minutes before serving. Garnish with basil, if desired.

Fried Green Tomatoes

Makes 6 to 8 servings

*"Don't skip salting the tomatoes. It draws out excess moisture
and helps keep the tomatoes from getting soggy after they're fried."—Paula*

5 green tomatoes, sliced
½ inch thick
1½ teaspoons salt, divided
1½ cups all-purpose flour,
divided
1 cup whole buttermilk
1 large egg
1 cup plain yellow cornmeal
1 tablespoon seasoned salt
Vegetable oil, for frying

1. Preheat oven to 200°. Line a large rimmed baking sheet with paper towels; place a wire rack on top.

2. Sprinkle both sides of all tomato slices with salt. Let stand for 30 minutes. Pat dry with paper towels.

3. In a shallow dish, place ½ cup flour. In another shallow dish, whisk together buttermilk and egg. In a third shallow dish, whisk together cornmeal, seasoned salt, and remaining 1 cup flour.

4. In a large skillet, pour oil to a depth of ⅛ inch, and heat over medium heat. Dredge tomatoes in flour, shaking off excess. Dip in buttermilk mixture, letting excess drip off. Dredge in cornmeal mixture, shaking off excess.

5. Fry tomatoes in batches until golden brown, 3 to 4 minutes per side. Let drain on prepared rack; keep warm in oven while frying remaining tomatoes.

Field Peas with Snaps

Makes about 6 cups

Throw in some shredded cooked chicken or turkey to turn this easy side into a hearty main dish.

¾ cup olive oil
¼ cup balsamic vinegar
3 tablespoons sugar
1 (16-ounce) package frozen
field peas with snaps, cooked
according to shortest time on
package and drained
1 large tomato, seeded and
chopped
½ cup chopped orange bell
pepper
½ cup chopped yellow bell
pepper
½ cup chopped green onion
¼ cup minced fresh parsley
1 tablespoon minced fresh
rosemary
½ teaspoon salt
½ teaspoon ground black pepper

1. In a large bowl, whisk together oil, vinegar, and sugar until dissolved. Stir in cooked peas and all remaining ingredients. Cover and refrigerate for at least 1 hour before serving.

Fried Okra

Makes 4 to 6 servings

Frying whole okra pods minimizes the "slime" that sometimes occurs with sliced okra, but you still get that unmistakeable crunch and great okra flavor.

3 cups plain cornmeal
1 cup all-purpose flour
2 tablespoons Cajun seasoning
2 teaspoons baking powder
2 teaspoons kosher salt
1 teaspoon ground black pepper
1 cup whole buttermilk
2 large eggs
Vegetable oil, for frying
1 pound whole fresh okra
Creamy Chive Sauce (recipe follows)

1. In a large bowl, whisk together cornmeal, flour, Cajun seasoning, baking powder, salt, and pepper. In another large bowl, whisk together buttermilk and eggs.

2. Preheat oven to 200°. Line a large rimmed baking sheet with paper towels; place a wire rack on top. In a large skillet, pour oil to a depth of 1½ inches, and heat over medium-high heat until a deep-fry thermometer registers 350°.

3. Working in batches, dip okra in buttermilk mixture, letting excess drip off. Dredge in cornmeal mixture, gently pressing to adhere. Fry until golden brown, about 2 minutes per side. Let drain on prepared rack, and keep warm in oven. Serve with Creamy Chive Sauce.

Creamy Chive Sauce

Makes about 1 cup

½ cup sour cream
¼ cup chopped fresh chives
¼ cup mayonnaise
2 teaspoons lemon zest
3 tablespoons fresh lemon juice
½ teaspoon kosher salt

1. In a small bowl, whisk together all ingredients. Cover and refrigerate for up to 3 days.

KITCHEN TIP

Buy tender but firm, brightly colored okra pods. If you can snap the pod in half, it's good. Avoid okra that looks dull, dry, or blemished. If you're lucky enough to have a Paula Deen Air Fryer, this is a great recipe to cook in it. If you don't have one, they are available at *evine.com*.

Creamy Smoky Mac and Cheese

Makes 8 to 10 servings

It's a good thing this recipe makes a lot of servings because you'll definitely want a second helping.

¼ cup unsalted butter

¼ cup all-purpose flour

4 cups whole milk

1½ teaspoons salt

1 teaspoon smoked paprika

½ teaspoon ground black pepper

2 cups shredded extra-sharp Cheddar cheese

1 cup diced processed cheese product

1 (16-ounce) package elbow macaroni, cooked according to package directions

Garnish: smoked paprika

1. In a large Dutch oven, melt butter over medium heat. Whisk in flour; cook for 1 minute. Gradually whisk in milk, salt, paprika, and pepper until smooth. Bring to a boil over medium-high heat, whisking constantly. Reduce heat, and simmer, whisking constantly, until thickened, about 2 minutes.

2. Gradually stir in cheeses until melted and smooth. Remove from heat, and stir in cooked pasta. Let stand for 5 minutes before serving; garnish with paprika, if desired.

Braised Collards with Country Ham

Makes 8 to 10 servings

"Don't forget a big piece of cornbread to soak up the potlikker."—Paula

1 tablespoon canola oil
1 (4-ounce) slice country ham, chopped
2 cloves garlic, minced
2 cups low-sodium chicken broth
⅓ cup apple cider vinegar
2 (16-ounce) packages chopped fresh collard greens
1 tablespoon sugar
2 teaspoons salt
1 teaspoon ground black pepper

1. In a large Dutch oven, heat oil over medium-high heat. Add ham; cook, stirring occasionally, until crisp, about 4 minutes. Add garlic; cook for 1 minute. Stir in broth and vinegar, scraping bottom of pot with a wooden spoon to loosen browned bits.

2. Stir in greens and sugar, and bring to a boil. Reduce heat, cover, and simmer, stirring occasionally, until greens are tender, about 30 minutes. Stir in salt and pepper.

Casseroles for a Crowd

ONE-DISH DINNERS

Y'all, I am crazy about casseroles. Even though I've been cooking for years, I've never stopped making these flavorful main-dish bakes that are easy enough for even the newest cooks to prepare. I've always loved their simplicity, and the flavor options are truly endless. These yummy recipes will have you pulling out your trusty 9x13s to make comforting meals for your family, to take to a potluck, or to give to a friend in need.

Homestyle Chicken Pot Pie

Makes 6 to 8 servings

This is classic comfort food that just can't be beat.

Crust:
1⅓ cups all-purpose flour
½ teaspoon salt
¼ teaspoon baking powder
¼ cup butter, cubed
¼ cup all-vegetable shortening, cubed
3 to 4 tablespoons ice water

Filling:
2 tablespoons butter
1 cup diced peeled baking potatoes
1 cup (1-inch pieces) fresh green beans
¾ cup fresh or thawed frozen corn kernels
½ cup chopped carrot
½ cup chopped onion
½ cup chopped celery
1¼ cups chicken broth
1 cup half-and-half
½ cup all-purpose flour
1 tablespoon chopped fresh parsley
1½ teaspoons salt, divided
½ teaspoon ground black pepper
½ teaspoon dried thyme
3 cups chopped cooked chicken
1 egg, beaten

1. For crust: In a large bowl, whisk together flour, salt, and baking powder. Using a pastry blender, cut in butter and shortening until mixture is crumbly. Stir in ice water 1 tablespoon at a time with a fork just until dry ingredients are moistened.

2. Turn out dough onto a lightly floured surface, and shape into a disk. Wrap in plastic wrap, and refrigerate for 30 minutes.

3. Preheat oven to 375°. Spray a 10-inch deep-dish pie plate with cooking spray.

4. For filling: In a large skillet, melt butter over medium heat. Add potatoes, beans, corn, carrot, onion, and celery; cook, stirring occasionally, until vegetables begin to soften, about 7 minutes.

5. In a small bowl, stir together broth and half-and-half; whisk in flour until mixture is smooth. Stir half-and-half mixture, parsley, 1¼ teaspoons salt, pepper, and thyme into vegetables, and bring to a boil over medium-high heat. Cook, stirring frequently, until sauce is thickened, 3 to 5 minutes. Remove from heat, and stir in chicken. Pour mixture into prepared pan.

6. On a lightly floured surface, roll dough to a 12-inch circle; place on top of chicken mixture. Fold edges of dough under, and crimp as desired. Cut 6 slits in top of dough to release steam. Brush beaten egg onto dough, and sprinkle with remaining ¼ teaspoon salt. Place pot pie on a rimmed baking sheet.

7. Bake until crust is golden brown and filling is hot and bubbly, about 40 minutes. Let stand for 10 minutes before serving.

Turkey Tetrazzini

Makes 6 to 8 servings

Tender turkey, flavorful veggies, and hearty pasta are smothered in a rich cream sauce in this filling casserole.

½ cup butter

1 (8-ounce) package sliced fresh baby portobello mushrooms

1 cup chopped onion

2 teaspoons minced garlic

⅓ cup all-purpose flour

1 tablespoon minced fresh thyme

½ teaspoon salt

¼ teaspoon ground black pepper

3 cups chicken broth

1 cup heavy whipping cream

3 cups shredded cooked turkey

1 (12-ounce) package frozen peas

1 (5-ounce) package shredded Parmesan cheese

1 (16-ounce) package rotini pasta, cooked according to package directions

¼ cup panko (Japanese bread crumbs)

2 teaspoons olive oil

1. Preheat oven to 350°. Spray a 3-quart baking dish with cooking spray.

2. In a large skillet, melt butter over medium heat. Add mushrooms, onion, and garlic; cook, stirring occasionally, until vegetables are tender, about 6 minutes. Stir in flour, thyme, salt, and pepper; cook, stirring constantly, for 2 minutes. Stir in broth and cream; cook, stirring frequently, until slightly thickened, about 10 minutes. Stir in turkey, peas, and cheese; cook for 5 minutes. Stir in cooked pasta. Pour mixture into prepared pan.

3. In a small bowl, stir together bread crumbs and oil; sprinkle onto casserole.

4. Bake until hot and bubbly and topping is golden brown, about 30 minutes. Let stand for 10 minutes before serving.

Kentucky Hot Brown Casserole

Makes 8 servings

If there were ever a sandwich that belonged in a casserole dish, it's the cheesy, gravy-smothered Hot Brown. Created by the chefs of Louisville's Brown Hotel in the 1920s to satisfy the demands of their late-night dancing guests, this classic sandwich begs to be eaten with a knife and fork.

¼ cup unsalted butter
¼ cup all-purpose flour
2½ cups whole milk
2 cups shredded Swiss cheese, divided
1 cup shredded extra-sharp white Cheddar cheese
1 teaspoon kosher salt
¼ teaspoon ground black pepper
8 slices thick sandwich bread, toasted
2 pounds thinly sliced turkey
¼ teaspoon paprika
8 slices bacon, cooked and halved crosswise
Chopped tomatoes
Garnish: fresh parsley

1. Preheat oven to broil. Spray a 13x9-inch baking dish with cooking spray.

2. In a medium saucepan, melt butter over medium heat. Whisk in flour; cook for 1 minute. Gradually whisk in milk; cook, whisking constantly, until thickened, about 6 minutes. Remove from heat, and whisk in 1 cup Swiss, Cheddar, salt, and pepper until melted.

3. Place bread in prepared pan, overlapping as needed to fit. Top with turkey, cheese sauce, and remaining 1 cup Swiss; sprinkle with paprika.

4. Broil until cheese is melted and lightly browned, about 4 minutes. Top with bacon and tomatoes. Garnish with parsley, if desired. Serve immediately.

KITCHEN TIP

This is a great recipe for a big crowd because it can easily be doubled or tripled. Assemble batches in disposable foil baking pans for easy cleanup.

Country Captain

Makes 4 to 6 servings

Sweet raisins play off spicy ground ginger and curry powder in this traditional rice-based Lowcountry casserole. Most agree that the recipe was brought over from India by a 19th century English skipper (hence the name), and it quickly gained a lot of fans, including President Franklin D. Roosevelt and General George Patton. Not only is this dish an American favorite, but it pays homage to the role of international spices in Southern cooking.

1 tablespoon vegetable oil

1½ cups frozen vegetable seasoning blend, thawed

1 (14.5-ounce) can diced tomatoes, undrained

½ cup golden raisins

½ cup unsalted chicken broth

1½ teaspoons salt

1½ teaspoons ground ginger

1½ teaspoons curry powder

½ teaspoon ground black pepper

2 cups shredded cooked chicken

2 cups long-grain rice, cooked according to package directions

½ cup sliced almonds

Garnish: chopped green onion

1. Preheat oven to 350°.

2. In a 10-inch enamel-coated cast-iron skillet, heat oil over medium-high heat. Add vegetable blend; cook until tender, about 5 minutes. Stir in tomatoes, raisins, broth, salt, ginger, curry, and pepper, and bring to a boil. Remove from heat, and stir in chicken and rice. Sprinkle with almonds.

3. Bake until almonds are lightly browned, about 30 minutes. Let stand for 5 minutes before serving. Garnish with green onion, if desired.

--- **KITCHEN TIP** ---

Pick up a rotisserie chicken and a few pouches
of fully cooked rice to make this recipe in no time.

Chicken Alfredo
Pasta Bake,
page 143

Chicken Alfredo Pasta Bake

Makes 6 to 8 servings

*It doesn't take much more effort than stirring the
ingredients together to assemble this creamy casserole.*

1 (16-ounce) box rigatoni pasta
2 cups small broccoli florets
2 (10-ounce) containers
  refrigerated alfredo sauce
1 (15-ounce) container ricotta
  cheese
1 (8-ounce) container sour
  cream
1 cup heavy whipping cream
2 large eggs
3 cups shredded rotisserie
  chicken
½ cup chopped red bell pepper
1½ cups shredded mozzarella
  cheese

1. Preheat oven to 350°. Spray a 3-quart baking dish with cooking spray.

2. Cook pasta according to package directions, adding broccoli during last 2 minutes of cooking. Drain well.

3. In a large bowl, whisk together alfredo sauce, ricotta, sour cream, heavy cream, and eggs until smooth; stir in chicken, bell pepper, and pasta mixture until well combined. Pour into prepared pan, and sprinkle with mozzarella.

4. Bake until golden brown and bubbly, about 45 minutes. Let stand for 10 minutes before serving.

──────────── KITCHEN TIP ────────────

The ridges of rigatoni really hold on to creamy sauces,
but any short tubular pasta you have on hand will work.

Baked Rigatoni and Cheese-Stuffed Meatballs

Makes 6 servings

These tender meatballs have a melty surprise inside that kids will just love.

1 (28-ounce) can crushed San Marzano tomatoes

½ cup shredded mozzarella cheese

½ (16-ounce) box rigatoni, cooked according to package directions

½ pound lean ground beef

½ pound ground Italian sausage

½ cup shredded Parmesan cheese, divided

¼ cup chopped fresh parsley

¼ cup dry bread crumbs

¼ cup whole milk

1 clove garlic, minced

1 teaspoon salt

½ teaspoon ground black pepper

1 large egg, lightly beaten

1 (4-ounce) package fresh mozzarella, cut into ½-inch pieces

Garnish: fresh basil

1. Preheat oven to 375°.

2. In a medium bowl, stir together tomatoes and shredded mozzarella. Spoon half of tomato mixture into an 11x9-inch baking dish. Spread cooked pasta onto tomato mixture; top with remaining tomato mixture.

3. In a large bowl, stir together beef, sausage, ¼ cup Parmesan, parsley, bread crumbs, milk, garlic, salt, pepper, and egg. Shape mixture into 2-inch balls. Press thumb in center of each meatball to make an indentation, and place one piece of fresh mozzarella in indentation. Shape meat around cheese to fully enclose, and place meatballs in sauce on top of pasta. Sprinkle with remaining ¼ cup Parmesan.

4. Bake until sauce is hot and bubbly and meatballs are cooked through, about 45 minutes. Let stand for 5 minutes before serving. Garnish with basil, if desired.

KITCHEN TIP

If you can't find San Marzano tomatoes, which are a variety of plum tomatoes, add a small pinch of sugar to regular canned tomatoes.

Individual Shepherd's Pies

Makes 6 to 8 servings

*Call all your meat-and-potatoes men to the dinner table with
these personal casseroles that are full of bold flavor.*

Filling:
- 1 tablespoon butter
- 1 (8-ounce) package fresh baby portobello mushrooms, quartered
- 1 cup diced peeled carrot
- 1 cup diced peeled parsnip
- ½ cup chopped yellow onion
- 2 cloves garlic, minced
- ½ teaspoon salt
- ½ teaspoon ground black pepper
- 3 pounds ground lamb
- ⅔ cup all-purpose flour
- 1 (12-ounce) bottle stout beer
- 1 cup beef broth
- 1 cup frozen peas

Topping:
- 3 pounds russet potatoes, peeled and cut into 1-inch pieces
- 4 teaspoons salt, divided
- 6 tablespoons butter, softened
- ¼ cup half-and-half
- 1 large egg
- 1 teaspoon minced garlic
- ½ teaspoon ground black pepper

Garnish: chopped fresh chives

1. Preheat oven to 350°. Spray 6 to 8 (2-cup) ramekins with cooking spray.

2. For filling: In a large skillet, melt butter over medium heat. Add mushrooms, carrot, parsnip, onion, garlic, salt, and pepper. Cook, stirring frequently, until mushrooms have released their liquid, about 10 minutes. Add lamb; cook, stirring frequently, until browned and crumbly, about 10 minutes. Sprinkle with flour; cook, stirring constantly, for 2 minutes. Stir in beer and broth; cook, stirring occasionally, until thickened, 5 to 6 minutes. Stir in peas. Divide meat mixture among prepared ramekins. Place ramekins on a large rimmed baking sheet.

3. For topping: In a large Dutch oven, bring potatoes, 3 teaspoons salt, and cold water to cover to a boil over medium-high heat. Reduce heat, and simmer until potatoes are tender, about 10 minutes.

4. Drain potatoes well, and return to pot. Add butter and half-and-half; beat with a mixer at medium speed until very smooth. Add egg, garlic, pepper, and remaining 1 teaspoon salt, beating until well combined. Spread mixture onto filling in ramekins.

5. Bake until topping is golden brown and filling is hot and bubbly, about 30 minutes. Let stand for 10 minutes before serving; garnish with chives, if desired.

KITCHEN TIP

If you prefer to make one large casserole, use a 4½-quart baking dish,
and bake until hot and bubbly, about 45 minutes.

Bacon–Pimiento Macaroni and Cheese

Makes 6 to 8 servings

*Forgo using pre-shredded cheese for this recipe, and spend a few minutes doing
it yourself. Your dish will have a creamier texture than if you use the bagged stuff, and
you'll also save money since blocks of cheese are more affordable than shredded.*

5   slices bacon, chopped
¼   cup butter
½   cup all-purpose flour
4   cups half-and-half
3   cups shredded smoked
    Cheddar cheese, divided
3   cups shredded Parmesan
    cheese, divided
2   (8-ounce) packages cream
    cheese, softened
½   teaspoon salt
¼   teaspoon ground red pepper
1   (16-ounce) box small penne
    pasta cooked according to
    package directions
1   (4-ounce) jar diced pimientos,
    drained
Garnish: sliced green onion

1. Preheat oven to broil. Spray 6 to 8 (2-cup) ramekins with cooking
spray.
2. In a large Dutch oven, cook bacon over medium heat until crisp.
Remove bacon using a slotted spoon, and let drain on paper towels,
reserving drippings in pot.
3. Melt butter with drippings in pot over medium-high heat. Whisk
in flour until smooth; cook, whisking constantly, for 1 minute.
Whisk in half-and-half until smooth; cook, whisking frequently,
until thickened. Stir in 2 cups each Cheddar and Parmesan, cream
cheese, salt, and red pepper until melted and smooth. Stir in cooked
pasta, pimientos, and bacon. Spoon mixture into prepared ramekins.
Sprinkle with remaining 1 cup each Cheddar and Parmesan.
4. Broil until cheese is melted and lightly browned, about 4 minutes.
Garnish with green onion, if desired. Serve immediately.

—————————————— **KITCHEN TIP** ——————————————

You'll get about 2 cups shredded cheese from an 8-ounce block.

Baked Shrimp and Grits

Makes 6 to 8 servings

Serve this savory casserole for brunch, lunch, or dinner.

2 quarts water
1 lemon, sliced
3 tablespoons Old Bay
   Seasoning
1 pound large fresh shrimp,
   peeled and deveined
2 cups chicken broth
2 cups whole milk
2 teaspoons salt
2 teaspoons butter
1 cup stone-ground grits
1 cup shredded Cheddar
   cheese
1 cup cherry tomatoes, halved
4 green onions, chopped
4 slices center-cut bacon,
   chopped and cooked
2 cloves garlic, minced
½ cup chopped fresh parsley
¼ cup shredded Parmesan
   cheese
Garnish: chopped fresh chives

1. Preheat oven to 350°. Spray a 13x9-inch baking dish with cooking spray.

2. In a large saucepan, bring 2 quarts water, lemon, and Old Bay to a boil over medium-high heat. Add shrimp, and cook until barely pink, about 1 minute. Drain immediately, and let cool enough to handle. Cut shrimp into bite-size pieces.

3. In a large saucepan, bring broth, milk, salt, and butter to a boil over medium-high heat. Gradually whisk in grits. Reduce heat and simmer, whisking occasionally, until grits are tender, about 30 minutes. Remove from heat, and stir in Cheddar, tomatoes, green onion, two-thirds of bacon, garlic, and parsley until well combined. Stir in shrimp. Pour mixture into prepared pan, and sprinkle with Parmesan and remaining bacon.

4. Bake until golden brown, about 30 minutes. Let stand for 5 minutes before serving. Garnish with chives, if desired.

KITCHEN TIP

Watch the shrimp carefully when it's in the saucepan so it does
not overcook; it will fully cook as the casserole bakes.

Turkey and Dressing

Makes 6 to 8 servings

*This hearty casserole transforms two Southern Thanksgiving
essentials into one comforting dish to enjoy all year long.*

Turkey:
- 1 (4½-pound) fresh or thawed frozen turkey breast
- 2 stalks celery, cut into 1-inch pieces
- 2 carrots, cut into 1-inch pieces
- 1 onion, quartered
- ¼ cup fresh parsley leaves
- 1 tablespoon black peppercorns
- 2 bay leaves
- 1 teaspoon salt

Dressing:
- ½ cup butter
- 2½ cups chopped onion
- 2½ cups chopped celery
- 1 tablespoon minced garlic
- 2 (6-ounce) packages buttermilk cornbread mix, baked according to package directions
- 6 frozen buttermilk biscuits, baked according to package directions
- 1 tablespoon poultry seasoning
- 1 teaspoon rubbed sage
- 1 teaspoon dried thyme leaves
- 2 large eggs, lightly beaten

Garnish: chopped fresh parsley, chopped fresh sage

1. For turkey: In a large stockpot, bring all ingredients and water to cover to a boil over high heat. Reduce heat, and simmer until turkey is cooked through, about 45 minutes. Remove from heat, and let stand for 30 minutes.

2. Remove turkey from broth, and let cool enough to handle. Shred meat, discarding skin and bones.

3. Strain broth through a fine-mesh sieve, discarding solids. Measure 5 cups broth for dressing; freeze remaining broth for another use.

4. Preheat oven to 350°. Spray a 13x9-inch baking dish with cooking spray.

5. For dressing: In a large skillet, melt butter over medium heat. Add onion, celery, and garlic; cook, stirring frequently, until very tender, about 10 minutes.

6. Crumble baked cornbread and biscuits into a large bowl; stir in cooked vegetables, shredded turkey, poultry seasoning, sage, and thyme. Stir in eggs. Gradually stir in reserved 5 cups broth just until dry ingredients are moistened. Spoon mixture into prepared pan.

7. Bake until center is set, 30 to 45 minutes. Let stand for 10 minutes before serving. Garnish with parsley and sage, if desired.

Cheesy Meat Lasagna

Makes 6 to 8 servings

This dish is a tasty way to clean out the crisper drawer of your fridge. Chop up any veggies you have on hand and throw them in with the meat mixture or tomato sauce.

1½ pounds ground round
½ teaspoon salt
½ teaspoon ground black pepper
1½ teaspoons extra-virgin olive oil
1 cup diced onion
1 cup diced green bell pepper
1 (24-ounce) jar mushroom marinara sauce, divided
1 (14.5-ounce) can fire-roasted diced tomatoes, drained
½ teaspoon dried Italian seasoning
1 (15-ounce) container ricotta cheese
1 cup small-curd cottage cheese
2 large eggs, lightly beaten
2 cups shredded mozzarella cheese
2 cups shredded Monterey Jack cheese
12 lasagna noodles, cooked until just tender
Garnish: chopped fresh parsley

1. Preheat oven to 350°. Spray a 13x9-inch baking dish with cooking spray.

2. In a large skillet, cook beef, salt, and pepper over medium-high heat, stirring frequently, until browned and crumbly. Drain well, and transfer to a bowl.

3. In same skillet, heat oil over medium heat. Add onion and bell pepper; cook, stirring occasionally, until tender, 6 to 8 minutes. Remove from heat, and stir in beef and ½ cup marinara sauce.

4. In a large bowl, stir together tomatoes, Italian seasoning, and remaining marinara sauce. In a medium bowl, stir together ricotta, cottage cheese, and eggs. In another medium bowl, stir together mozzarella and Monterey Jack cheeses.

5. Spread ½ cup tomato mixture in bottom of prepared pan, and top with 4 lasagna noodles. Spread one-third of ricotta mixture onto noodles, and sprinkle with 1 cup shredded cheese mixture. Top cheese with one-third of beef mixture and one-third of tomato mixture. Starting with noodles, repeat layers twice. Spray a large piece of foil with cooking spray, and cover lasagna, spray side down.

6. Bake for 45 minutes. Uncover and sprinkle with remaining 1 cup cheese mixture. Bake until hot and bubbly and cheese is melted, 10 to 15 minutes more. Let stand for 10 minutes before serving. Garnish with parsley, if desired.

—————————————— **KITCHEN TIP** ——————————————

Oven-ready lasagna noodles can be used for faster assembly.

Baked Enchilada Pie

Makes 4 to 6 servings

This easy recipe gives you layer upon layer of delicious Tex-Mex goodness.

1 pound ground beef
1 (1.25-ounce) package taco seasoning
2 tablespoons butter
1 medium onion, chopped
2 tablespoons minced garlic
½ cup chopped green onion
1 (4-ounce) can chopped green chiles, drained
1 (10.75-ounce) can cream of onion soup
1 (16-ounce) can refried beans
1 cup red enchilada sauce
5 (12-inch) flour tortillas
2½ cups shredded Monterey Jack cheese with peppers
Garnish: chopped green onion, chopped tomatoes

1. Preheat oven to 350°.

2. In a 12-inch cast-iron skillet, cook beef and taco seasoning over medium heat, stirring frequently, until browned and crumbly; drain. Transfer to a large bowl.

3. In same skillet, melt butter. Add onion, garlic, and green onion; cook until tender, about 5 minutes. Stir in green chiles and soup until well combined. Stir onion mixture into beef mixture in bowl.

4. Wipe skillet clean with a paper towel. Lightly spray skillet with cooking spray. In a medium bowl, stir together beans and enchilada sauce until well combined.

5. Add 1 tortilla to skillet, and top with half of meat mixture. Top meat mixture with 1 tortilla and half of bean mixture. Repeat layers once, and top with remaining tortilla. Sprinkle with cheese.

6. Bake until hot and bubbly, about 30 minutes. Let stand for 10 minutes before serving. Garnish with green onion and tomato, if desired.

KITCHEN TIP

Fajita seasoning and green enchilada sauce can be used
instead of taco seasoning and red enchilada sauce.

Somethin' Sweet

DESSERTS

I just love dessert. Sweets have a magical quality about them, and they can take you way back in time to a special place, memory, or moment. I remember as a girl in Albany, Georgia, rushing home after school knowing that Mama would have a warm banana pudding with meringue sitting on the stovetop for my brother and me. It was so good! Today the sight of a baked 'nana puddin' brings back warm memories of my family and childhood simplicity. I hope these recipes inspire you to bake up some memories of your own.

Fresh Apple Cake with Praline Sauce

Makes 1 (10-inch) cake

Apples don't always have to be put into pie—give this cake a try. The nutty sauce makes this cake truly special, but work fast. It firms up as quickly as it cools, so be sure to spoon it on when it's warm.

2 cups sugar

1½ cups vegetable oil

4 large eggs

1 teaspoon vanilla extract

2½ cups all-purpose flour

2 teaspoons baking powder

1 teaspoon salt

1 teaspoon ground cinnamon

3 cups chopped peeled apples

1 cup chopped pecans

Praline Sauce (recipe follows)

1. Preheat oven to 350°. Spray a 12- to 15-cup Bundt pan with baking spray with flour.

2. In a large bowl, beat sugar and oil with a mixer at medium speed until combined. Add eggs, one at a time, beating well after each addition. Beat in vanilla.

3. In another large bowl, whisk together flour, baking powder, salt, and cinnamon. Gradually add flour mixture to sugar mixture, beating until combined. Stir in apples and pecans. Pour batter into prepared pan.

4. Bake until a wooden pick inserted near center comes out clean, about 70 minutes. Let cool in pan for 20 minutes. Remove from pan, and let cool completely on a wire rack.

5. Spoon warm Praline Sauce onto cooled cake; let stand for 10 minutes before serving. Store in an airtight container for up to 3 days.

Praline Sauce

Makes about 1½ cups

1½ cups firmly packed light brown sugar

½ cup butter

½ cup chopped pecans

1 tablespoon whole milk

1. In a small saucepan, bring all ingredients to a boil over medium-high heat. Cook, stirring occasionally, until a candy thermometer registers 234°. Remove from heat, and let cool for 10 minutes; use immediately.

Sweet Potato Pie with Swiss Meringue

Makes 1 (9-inch) deep-dish pie

The fluffy Swiss Meringue topping takes this classic Southern pie to the next level.

½ (14.1-ounce) package refrigerated piecrusts

2 large eggs

2 cups mashed cooked sweet potato

1 cup evaporated milk

⅓ cup firmly packed light brown sugar

2 tablespoons unsalted butter, melted

2 tablespoons unsulphured molasses

1 tablespoon all-purpose flour

1 teaspoon vanilla extract

¾ teaspoon kosher salt

½ teaspoon ground cinnamon

½ teaspoon orange zest

Swiss Meringue (recipe follows)

1. Preheat oven to 350°.

2. On a lightly floured surface, unroll pie crust, and roll to a 12-inch circle. Press into bottom and up sides of a 9-inch deep-dish pie plate. Fold edges under, and crimp as desired. Line crust with parchment paper, letting ends extend over sides of crust; add pie weights.

3. Bake until lightly browned, about 15 minutes. Carefully remove weights and parchment, and let crust cool completely. Leave oven on.

4. In a large bowl, whisk together eggs, sweet potato, milk, brown sugar, melted butter, molasses, flour, vanilla, salt, cinnamon, and zest until smooth; pour into cooled crust.

5. Bake until center is set, 30 to 40 minutes, loosely covering with foil to prevent excess browning, if necessary. Let cool completely in pan on a wire rack.

6. Preheat oven to broil.

7. Spread Swiss Meringue on top of cooled pie, and broil until meringue is lightly browned, about 30 seconds. Let cool before serving.

Swiss Meringue

Makes about 3½ cups

1 cup sugar

⅛ teaspoon cream of tartar

3 large egg whites

1. In the top of a double boiler, whisk together sugar, cream of tartar, and egg whites. Cook over simmering water, whisking constantly, until sugar is dissolved and mixture registers 140° on a candy thermometer, 3 to 4 minutes.

2. Remove from heat, and pour mixture into the bowl of a stand mixer fitted with the whisk attachment. Beat at high speed until mixture is stiff, glossy, and cool to the touch, about 7 minutes.

Coconut Pecan Pie

Makes 1 (9-inch) pie

Coconut is a sweet and chewy addition to classic pecan pie.

½ (14.1-ounce) package refrigerated piecrusts

2 large eggs

½ cup firmly packed light brown sugar

⅓ cup light corn syrup

¼ cup unsalted butter, melted

½ teaspoon kosher salt

½ teaspoon vanilla extract

⅛ teaspoon ground cinnamon

1 cup chopped pecans

½ cup sweetened flaked coconut

1. Preheat oven to 350°.

2. On a lightly floured surface, roll piecrust to a 12-inch circle. Press into bottom and up sides of a 9-inch pie plate or cast-iron skillet. Fold edges under, and crimp as desired.

3. In a large bowl, whisk together eggs, brown sugar, corn syrup, melted butter, salt, vanilla, and cinnamon until well combined. Stir in pecans and coconut. Pour into prepared crust.

4. Bake until crust is golden brown and center is set, about 30 minutes. Let cool completely. Store in an airtight container, covered, for up to 2 days.

Peach Cobbler

Makes 8 to 10 servings

*"As a Georgia gal, y'all know I'm partial to peaches,
and the buttery crust on top of the peach filling is fantastic."—Paula*

1 cup unsalted butter, softened
1⅔ cups sugar, divided
2 large eggs
3 cups all-purpose flour
½ teaspoon salt
12 cups sliced peeled fresh peaches (about 6 pounds)
3 tablespoons fresh lemon juice
¼ cup cornstarch

1. In a large bowl, beat butter and ⅔ cup sugar with a mixer at medium speed until creamy, 3 to 4 minutes, stopping to scrape bowl. Add eggs, one at a time, beating well after each addition. Gradually beat in flour and salt until smooth, stopping to scrape bowl (dough will be thick).

2. Turn out dough onto a lightly floured surface, and shape into a rectangle. Wrap in plastic wrap, and refrigerate for 30 minutes.

3. In a large bowl, stir together peaches, ¾ cup sugar, and lemon juice; let stand while dough chills.

4. Preheat oven to 375°. Spray a 13x9-inch baking dish with cooking spray.

5. Drain peaches, discarding liquid; stir in cornstarch and remaining ¼ cup sugar until well combined. Pour into prepared pan. On a lightly floured surface, roll dough to a 14x10-inch rectangle, about ¼ inch thick. Place on peaches, and fold excess dough around edges. Cut slits in dough to let steam escape.

6. Bake until crust is golden brown and filling is hot and bubbly, 40 to 45 minutes. Let cool for at least 30 minutes before serving.

Classic Banana Pudding

Makes about 12 servings

"I'll always have a special place in my heart for banana pudding with a cooked custard and meringue. It's still one of my absolute favorite comfort foods."—Paula

1¾ **cups sugar, divided**
½ **cup all-purpose flour**
¼ **teaspoon kosher salt**
3½ **cups whole milk, divided**
6 **large eggs, separated**
1 **tablespoon unsalted butter**
1½ **teaspoons vanilla extract**
1 **(11-ounce) box vanilla wafers**
6 **medium bananas, sliced**
¾ **teaspoon cream of tartar**

1. Preheat oven to 375°.

2. In a medium bowl, whisk together 1 cup sugar, flour, and salt. Whisk in ½ cup milk and egg yolks until smooth.

3. In a large saucepan, cook remaining 3 cups milk over medium heat, stirring frequently, just until bubbles form around sides of pan. Gradually whisk 1 cup hot milk into egg mixture. Whisk egg mixture into remaining hot milk in pan. Cook, whisking constantly, until thickened, 3 to 5 minutes. Remove from heat; whisk in butter and vanilla until melted.

4. Reserve 1 cup vanilla wafers; arrange remaining vanilla wafers in bottom of a 13x9-inch baking dish. Top with bananas; spread pudding onto bananas.

5. In a large bowl, beat egg whites and cream of tartar with a mixer at medium speed until soft peaks form. Increase speed to high; gradually add remaining ¾ cup sugar, beating until stiff peaks form. Spread onto pudding, sealing edges.

6. Bake until top is lightly browned, about 7 minutes. Arrange reserved 1 cup wafers around sides of dish. Let stand for 10 minutes before serving.

———— KITCHEN TIP ————

It's best to serve this pudding soon after the meringue is baked. If it's refrigerated, the meringue will start to become soggy and weep.

Birthday Cake Cookies
Makes about 42

"My grandson Jack loves confetti cupcakes, so I came up with these cookies for him. We have such a good time in the kitchen when he helps me make 'em."—Paula

1   **cup butter, softened**
2   **cups sugar, divided**
2   **large eggs**
1½ **teaspoons vanilla extract**
1   **teaspoon almond extract**
3   **cups all-purpose flour**
2   **teaspoons baking powder**
2   **teaspoons cream of tartar**
1   **teaspoon baking soda**
1   **teaspoon salt**
2   **tablespoons heavy whipping cream**
1   **cup rainbow sprinkles**

1. In a large bowl, beat butter and 1⅓ cups sugar with a mixer at medium-high speed until fluffy, 3 to 4 minutes, stopping occasionally to scrape sides of bowl. Add eggs, one at a time, beating until combined after each addition. Beat in extracts.

2. In a medium bowl, whisk together flour, baking powder, cream of tartar, baking soda, and salt. Gradually add flour mixture to butter mixture, beating just until combined. Add cream, beating just until combined. Beat in sprinkles. Cover dough with plastic wrap, and refrigerate for at least 1 hour or for up to 3 days.

3. Preheat oven to 350°. Line baking sheets with parchment paper.

4. Place remaining ⅔ cup sugar in a small bowl. Using a 1-inch spring-loaded ice cream scoop, scoop dough into balls, and roll in sugar to coat. Place 2 inches apart on prepared pans.

5. Bake until edges are lightly browned, about 10 minutes. Let cool on pans for 5 minutes. Remove from pans, and let cool completely on wire racks. Store in an airtight container for up to 5 days.

Chocolate Gooey Butter Cake Bars
Makes about 24

"I've made my gooey butter cake in just about every flavor I can think of. Fruit flavors are great for spring and summer, and in the fall and winter I make 'em with pumpkin and spice cake mixes. But chocolate works all year, and with my Double Chocoate Ooey Gooey Butter Cake Mix, you can whip up these treats in no time."—Paula

1   **(15.25-ounce) box dark chocolate cake mix**
3   **large eggs, divided**
1   **cup butter, melted and divided**
1   **(8-ounce) package cream cheese, softened**
1   **teaspoon vanilla extract**
1   **(16-ounce) package confectioners' sugar**
Garnish: confectioners' sugar

1. Preheat oven to 350°. Line a 13x9-inch baking pan with parchment paper, letting excess extend over sides of pan.

2. In a large bowl, beat cake mix, 1 egg, and ½ cup melted butter with a mixer at medium speed just until combined. Pat mixture into bottom of prepared pan.

3. In another large bowl, beat cream cheese with a mixer at medium speed until smooth. Beat in vanilla and remaining 2 eggs. Reduce speed to low; beat in confectioners' sugar until well combined. Slowly add remaining ½ cup melted butter, beating until well combined. Pour onto crust in prepared pan.

4. Bake until center is just set and jiggles slightly when gently shaken, 40 to 50 minutes (do not overbake). Let cool completely on a wire rack. Using excess parchment as handles, remove from pan before cutting into bars. Garnish with confectioners' sugar, if desired. Store in an airtight container for up to 2 days.

Luscious Lemon Cake,
page 173

Luscious Lemon Cake

Makes 1 (9-inch) cake

The lemon filling and fluffy frosting are extra-special touches that make this cake truly scrumptious.

Filling:
- ¾ cup water, divided
- 1 (0.25-ounce) envelope unflavored gelatin
- 1 cup sugar
- 3 tablespoons cornstarch
- 8 large egg yolks
- 1 cup fresh lemon juice
- ¼ cup butter, cubed

Cake:
- 1½ cups unsalted butter, softened
- 2 cups sugar
- 1 tablespoon lemon zest
- 1 teaspoon vanilla extract
- 3½ cups cake flour
- 1 tablespoon baking powder
- ½ teaspoon baking soda
- ¼ teaspoon salt
- 1¼ cups whole buttermilk
- ½ cup sour cream
- 8 large eggs whites

Frosting:
- ¾ cup butter, softened
- 3 tablespoons heavy whipping cream
- 1 tablespoon lemon zest
- 5 cups confectioners' sugar
- 1 (12-ounce) container frozen whipped topping, thawed

Garnish: fresh lemon wedges, lemon zest strips

1. For filling: In a small bowl, stir together ¼ cup water and gelatin; let stand until softened, about 5 minutes.

2. In a medium heavy-bottomed saucepan, whisk together sugar and cornstarch. Whisk in egg yolks, lemon juice, and remaining ½ cup water until smooth. Cook over medium heat, whisking constantly, until thickened, 4 to 5 minutes. Remove from heat, and whisk in gelatin mixture and butter until melted and smooth.

3. Pour mixture into a medium bowl, and cover with plastic wrap, pressing wrap directly on surface to prevent a skin from forming. Refrigerate for at least 8 hours before using or up to overnight.

4. Preheat oven to 350°. Spray 3 (9-inch) round cake pans with baking spray with flour.

5. For cake: In a large bowl, beat butter, sugar, zest, and vanilla with a mixer at medium speed until fluffy, 4 to 5 minutes, stopping to scrape bowl.

6. In another large bowl, sift together flour, baking powder, baking soda, and salt. Gradually add flour mixture to butter mixture alternately with buttermilk, beginning and ending with flour mixture, beating just until combined after each addition. Stir in sour cream.

7. In a third large bowl, beat egg whites with a mixer at high speed until stiff peaks form. Gently fold egg whites into batter. Divide batter among prepared pans.

8. Bake until a wooden pick inserted in center comes out clean, 15 to 20 minutes. Let cool in pans for 10 minutes. Remove from pans, and let cool completely on wire racks.

9. For frosting: In a large bowl, beat butter, cream, and zest with a mixer at medium speed until smooth. Gradually add confectioners' sugar, beating until smooth. Beat in whipped topping until smooth.

10. Place one cake layer on a serving plate, and spread with half of filling. Repeat layers, and top with remaining cake layer. Spread frosting on top and sides of cake. Garnish with lemon wedges and strips, if desired. Cover and refrigerate for up to 3 days.

Peanut Butter Pie

Makes 1 (9-inch) pie

This rich, creamy, sweet, and indulgent pie is a peanut butter lover's dream.

2 cups vanilla wafer crumbs
¼ cup firmly packed light brown sugar
⅓ cup butter, melted
1 cup semisweet chocolate morsels
½ cup heavy whipping cream
2 tablespoons confectioners' sugar
1 (8-ounce) package cream cheese, softened
¾ cup crunchy peanut butter
1 (14-ounce) can sweetened condensed milk
Garnish: grated chocolate, sweetened whipped cream, fresh strawberries

1. Preheat oven to 350°.
2. In a medium bowl, stir together wafer crumbs, brown sugar, and melted butter until well combined. Press into bottom and up sides of a 9-inch pie plate.
3. Bake for 8 minutes. Sprinkle chocolate morsels onto hot crust; let stand for 2 minutes. Spread chocolate evenly onto crust.
4. In a small bowl, beat heavy cream with a mixer at medium speed until soft peaks form. Gradually add confectioners' sugar, beating until stiff peaks form; refrigerate.
5. In a large bowl, beat cream cheese and peanut butter with a mixer at medium speed until creamy. Beat in condensed milk until well combined; gently fold in whipped cream. Spread mixture into prepared crust. Cover and refrigerate overnight before serving. Garnish with chocolate, whipped cream, and strawberries, if desired.

Giant Chocolate Chip Cookies

Makes about 18

Don't skip lining your baking sheets with parchment paper; the cookies will definitely stick to the pans if you don't, even if they're sprayed with cooking spray.

1½ cups butter, softened
1¾ cups firmly packed light brown sugar
½ cup granulated sugar
1 tablespoon vanilla extract
3 large eggs
3½ cups all-purpose flour
1 teaspoon baking powder
1 teaspoon salt
½ teaspoon baking soda
1 (11.5-ounce) package semisweet chocolate chunks
1 cup miniature semisweet chocolate morsels

1. In a large bowl, beat butter, sugars, and vanilla with a mixer at medium-high speed until fluffy, 4 to 5 minutes, stopping to scrape bowl. Add eggs, one at a time, beating well after each addition.
2. In another large bowl, whisk together flour, baking powder, salt, and baking soda. Gradually add flour mixture to butter mixture, beating just until combined. Stir in all chocolate. Cover and refrigerate dough for at least 2 hours or up to overnight.
3. Preheat oven to 350°. Line baking sheets with parchment paper.
4. Scoop dough by ½ cupfuls onto prepared pans. Bake until center of cookies is just set, about 18 minutes. Let cool on pans for 5 minutes. Remove from pans, and let cool completely on wire racks. Store in an airtight container for up to 5 days.

Mississippi Mud Brownies

Makes about 24

Call your kids or grandkids into the kitchen to help you make these goodies.

Brownie:
- 1 cup butter, melted
- 1¾ cups sugar
- 4 large eggs
- 1 teaspoon vanilla extract
- 1½ cups all-purpose flour
- ½ cup unsweetened cocoa powder
- 2 teaspoons baking powder
- ½ teaspoon salt
- ¾ cup creamy peanut butter
- 2 cups miniature marshmallows
- 1 cup chopped toasted pecans

Frosting:
- ½ cup butter, melted
- 5 tablespoons unsweetened cocoa powder
- ⅓ cup whole milk
- 1 teaspoon vanilla extract
- 3 cups confectioners' sugar

1. Preheat oven to 350°. Line a 13x9-inch baking pan with foil, letting excess extend over sides of pan.

2. For brownie: In a large bowl, whisk together melted butter, sugar, eggs, and vanilla until smooth.

3. In a medium bowl, whisk together flour, cocoa, baking powder, and salt. Gradually whisk flour mixture into butter mixture until smooth. Spread batter into prepared pan.

4. Bake until a wooden pick inserted in center comes out clean, 20 to 25 minutes. Let cool for 10 minutes. Spread peanut butter onto warm brownie; sprinkle with marshmallows and pecans. Bake 4 minutes more. Let cool completely in pan.

5. For frosting: In a medium bowl, whisk together melted butter and cocoa until smooth. Whisk in milk and vanilla until combined. Gradually whisk in confectioners' sugar until smooth. Spread onto marshmallow layer. Cover and refrigerate until set, about 30 minutes.

6. Using excess foil as handles, remove from pan before cutting into squares. Store in an airtight container for up to 2 days.

Orange Buttermilk Pie

Makes 1 (9-inch) deep-dish pie

This pie is perfect for folks who prefer their desserts a little less sweet.

Crust:
1½ cups all-purpose flour
 1 tablespoon sugar
 1 teaspoon kosher salt
½ cup cold unsalted butter, cubed
5 to 6 tablespoons ice water

Filling:
 2 cups sugar
1½ cups whole buttermilk
¾ cup unsalted butter, melted
 5 large eggs
 5 tablespoons all-purpose flour
 4 teaspoons orange zest
 5 tablespoons fresh orange juice
 1 teaspoon vanilla extract

Sweetened whipped cream
Garnish: orange slices

1. For crust: In the work bowl of a food processor, pulse together flour, sugar, and salt. Add butter, and pulse until mixture is crumbly. Add ice water, 1 tablespoon at a time, pulsing just until dough comes together.

2. Turn out dough onto a lightly floured surface, and shape into a disk. Wrap in plastic wrap, and refrigerate for 2 hours.

3. On a lightly floured surface, roll dough to a 12-inch circle. Press into bottom and up sides of a 9-inch deep-dish pie plate. Fold edges under, and crimp as desired. Refrigerate for 30 minutes.

4. Preheat oven to 350°.

5. For filling: In a large bowl, whisk together sugar, buttermilk, melted butter, eggs, flour, orange zest and juice, and vanilla until smooth. Pour into prepared crust.

6. Bake until just set, 45 to 50 minutes, covering with foil halfway through baking time to prevent excess browning. Let cool completely on a wire rack. Top with whipped cream just before serving, and garnish with orange, if desired. Cover and refrigerate for up to 1 day.

———— KITCHEN TIP ————

To make sweetened whipped cream, beat 1 cup cold heavy whipping cream and
2 tablespoons confectioners' sugar with a mixer at high speed until soft peaks form.

Key Lime Pie

Makes 1 (9-inch) pie

The trick to the best Key Lime Pie is using real Key limes.
They are less tart than regular limes and are smaller in size.

1 sleeve unsalted saltine crackers
¼ cup sugar
½ cup unsalted butter, melted
1 (14-ounce) can sweetened condensed milk
¼ cup sour cream
½ teaspoon Key lime zest
½ cup fresh Key lime juice
3 large egg yolks
Sweetened whipped cream
Garnish: Key lime slices and zest

1. Preheat oven to 350°.

2. In the work bowl of a food processor, pulse together crackers and sugar until finely ground. Add melted butter, pulsing to combine. Press mixture into bottom and up sides of a 9-inch pie plate. Freeze for 10 minutes.

3. Bake for 12 minutes. Let cool completely. Leave oven on.

4. In a large bowl, whisk together condensed milk, sour cream, lime zest and juice, and egg yolks until smooth. Pour mixture into prepared crust.

5. Bake until center is set, about 15 minutes. Let cool completely. Refrigerate for at least 3 hours before serving or for up to 2 days. Top with whipped cream just before serving. Garnish with Key lime, if desired.

Perfect Pound Cake

Makes 1 (10-inch) cake

*"I like to spread a little butter on a toasted slice of pound cake.
If you've never tried that, you don't know what you're missing!"—Paula*

1 cup butter, softened
1 (8-ounce) package cream
  cheese, softened
3 cups granulated sugar
1 tablespoon vanilla extract
6 large eggs
3½ cups all-purpose flour
1 teaspoon baking powder
½ teaspoon salt
1 cup heavy whipping cream
Garnish: confectioners' sugar

1. Preheat oven to 325°. Spray a 12- to 15-cup Bundt pan with baking spray with flour.

2. In a large bowl, beat butter, cream cheese, granulated sugar, and vanilla with a mixer at medium speed until fluffy, stopping to scrape bowl. Add eggs, one at a time, beating well after each addition.

3. In a medium bowl, whisk together flour, baking powder, and salt. Gradually add flour mixture to butter mixture alternately with cream, beginning and ending with flour mixture, beating just until combined after each addition. Spoon batter into prepared pan.

4. Bake until a wooden pick inserted near center comes out clean, about 75 minutes, loosely covering with foil halfway through baking to prevent excess browning, if necessary. Let cool in pan for 20 minutes. Remove from pan, and let cool completely on a wire rack. Garnish with confectioners' sugar, if desired. Store in an airtight container for up to 3 days.

Caramel Layer Cake

Makes 1 (9-inch) cake

This is a great cake for any occasion and is always impressive.

Cake:
- 1 cup butter, softened
- 2 cups sugar
- 4 large eggs
- 1½ teaspoons vanilla extract
- 3 cups self-rising flour
- 1 cup whole buttermilk

Frosting:
- 2 cups granulated sugar
- ¼ cup water
- 2 tablespoons light corn syrup
- 1½ cups butter, softened and divided
- 1 cup heavy whipping cream
- 6 cups confectioners' sugar, sifted

Garnish: pecan halves

1. Preheat oven to 350°. Spray 3 (9-inch) round cake pans with baking spray with flour. Line bottom of pans with parchment paper; spray paper.

2. For cake: In a large bowl, beat butter and sugar with a mixer at medium speed until fluffy, 3 to 4 minutes, stopping to scrape bowl. Add eggs, one at a time, beating well after each addition. Beat in vanilla.

3. Gradually add flour to butter mixture alternately with buttermilk, beginning and ending with flour, beating just until combined after each addition. Divide batter among prepared pans.

4. Bake until a wooden pick inserted in center comes out clean, 25 to 30 minutes. Let cool in pans for 10 minutes. Remove from pans, and let cool completely on wire racks; gently remove parchment.

5. For frosting: In a large heavy-bottomed saucepan, whisk together granulated sugar, ¼ cup water, and corn syrup just until sugar is moistened. Cook, without stirring, over medium-high heat until mixture is golden brown. (While caramel cooks, brush any sugar crystals on sides of pan with a pastry brush dipped in water.)

6. Remove from heat, and carefully stir in ½ cup butter until melted. Slowly stir in cream until smooth. Let cool, stirring occasionally, until barely warm, about 1 hour. Reserve ⅓ cup caramel in a small bowl.

7. In a large bowl, beat remaining caramel and remaining 1 cup butter with a mixer at medium speed until smooth, stopping to scrape bowl. Gradually add confectioners' sugar, beating until smooth. Cover with plastic wrap, and let stand until frosting has reached a spreadable consistency, about 10 minutes.

8. Spread frosting between layers and on top and sides of cake. Drizzle with reserved ⅓ cup caramel, and garnish with pecans, if desired. Store in an airtight container for up to 2 days.

Coconut Sheet Cake

Makes 1 (13x9-inch) cake

Beaten egg whites folded into the batter make this cake light and fluffy.

Cake:
- 1 **cup unsalted butter, softened**
- 1½ **cups sugar**
- 4 **large eggs, separated**
- 1 **teaspoon vanilla extract**
- 1 **teaspoon coconut extract**
- 3 **cups cake flour**
- 1 **teaspoon baking powder**
- 1 **teaspoon baking soda**
- ½ **teaspoon salt**
- 1¼ **cups canned coconut milk**

Frosting:
- ¾ **cup butter, softened**
- 5 **tablespoons canned coconut milk**
- 1 **teaspoon coconut extract**
- 7 **cups confectioners' sugar**
- 1 **cup toasted sweetened flaked coconut**

1. Preheat oven to 350°. Spray a 13x9-inch baking dish with cooking spray.

2. For cake: In a large bowl, beat butter and sugar with a mixer at medium speed until fluffy, 3 to 4 minutes, stopping to scrape bowl. Add egg yolks, one at a time, beating well after each addition. Beat in extracts.

3. In another large bowl, sift together flour, baking powder, baking soda, and salt. Gradually add flour mixture to butter mixture alternately with coconut milk, beginning and ending with flour mixture, beating just until combined after each addition.

4. In a medium bowl, beat egg whites with a mixer at high speed just until stiff peaks form. Fold egg whites into batter. Gently spread batter into prepared pan.

5. Bake until a wooden pick inserted in center comes out clean, 25 to 30 minutes. Let cool completely.

6. For frosting: In a large bowl, beat butter, coconut milk, and extract with a mixer at medium speed until creamy. Gradually add confectioners' sugar, beating until smooth. Spread onto cake, and sprinkle with coconut. Cover and refrigerate for up to 3 days.

KITCHEN TIP

Give your can of coconut milk a good shake before measuring. To toast coconut, cook it in a dry skillet over medium heat, stirring frequently, until lightly browned.

Cherry Vanilla Ice Cream

Makes about 3 quarts

No need for a cherry on top of this fun summer treat—they're mixed right in.

3 cups whole milk

2 cups sugar

1 vanilla bean, split lengthwise, seeds scraped and reserved

4 large eggs

½ teaspoon salt

1 (12-ounce) can evaporated milk, chilled

2 cups chopped drained maraschino cherries

1. In a large saucepan, cook milk, sugar, vanilla bean, and reserved seeds over medium-low heat, stirring occasionally, just until bubbles form around sides of pan.

2. In a large bowl, whisk together eggs. Slowly whisk one-fourth of hot milk mixture into eggs. Whisk egg mixture into remaining milk mixture in pan. Cook, whisking constantly, over low heat until mixture thickens and coats the back of a spoon, 5 to 7 minutes. Strain mixture through a fine-mesh sieve into a large bowl, discarding solids. Stir in salt. Cover and refrigerate overnight.

3. Pour cold milk mixture into container of an electric ice cream maker, and add evaporated milk. Freeze according to manufacturer's instructions, adding cherries when mixture is partially frozen.

4. Transfer ice cream to a freezer-safe container, and freeze until firm before serving, at least 2 hours or for up to 2 weeks.

Pecan Pralines

Makes about 12

"Pralines are such a popular treat in Savannah, and they're easy enough to make at home any time you get a craving for them."—Paula

1½ cups firmly packed light brown sugar

½ cup heavy whipping cream

1 tablespoon light corn syrup

¼ teaspoon salt

2 tablespoons unsalted butter

1 cup chopped pecans

½ teaspoon vanilla extract

1. Line a large rimmed baking sheet with wax paper; spray paper with cooking spray.

2. In a large heavy-bottomed saucepan, stir together brown sugar, cream, corn syrup, and salt. Bring to a boil over medium heat, stirring until sugar is dissolved. Cook, stirring occasionally, until mixture registers 236° on a candy thermometer.

3. Remove from heat, and place butter in center of mixture (do not stir). Let stand until mixture registers 150° on a candy thermometer. Using a wooden spoon, stir in pecans and vanilla. Stir constantly until candy begins to thicken, 4 to 5 minutes. Working quickly, drop by rounded tablespoonfuls onto prepared pan. Let stand until firm. Store in an airtight container for up to 5 days.

Strawberry Lime Bars

Makes about 12

*Lime might not be an obvious flavor to pair with strawberries,
but it really brings out the natural sweetness of the berries.*

8 cups chopped fresh
   strawberries
1¾ cups sugar, divided
1 cup plus 3 tablespoons
   unsalted butter, softened
1 large egg yolk
2 cups all-purpose flour
⅔ cup old-fashioned oats
1½ teaspoons baking powder
½ teaspoon salt
2 tablespoons cornstarch
1 tablespoon lime zest
1 tablespoon fresh lime juice

1. Preheat oven to 375°. Spray a 13x9-inch baking pan with baking spray with flour. Line pan with parchment paper, letting excess extend over sides of pan.

2. In a large bowl, gently stir together strawberries and ½ cup sugar; let stand for 10 to 15 minutes.

3. Meanwhile, in another large bowl, beat butter and egg yolk with a mixer at medium speed until smooth and creamy. In a third large bowl, whisk together flour, 1 cup sugar, oats, baking powder, and salt. Gradually add flour mixture to butter mixture, beating just until combined. Turn out mixture onto a surface, and gently knead until a crumbly dough forms. Press three-fourths of dough into prepared pan; reserve remaining dough.

4. Drain strawberries, discarding liquid. Stir cornstarch, lime zest and juice, and remaining ¼ cup sugar into berries. Pour berries onto dough in pan; crumble reserved dough onto berries.

5. Bake until top is lightly browned and filling is hot and bubbly, about 45 minutes. Let cool completely in pan on a wire rack. Using excess parchment as handles, remove from pan before cutting into bars. Store in an airtight container for up to 2 days.

. VARIATION .
Blueberry Lemon Bars

Prepare dough and pat into baking pan as directed. In a large bowl, stir together 8 cups fresh blueberries, 1 cup sugar, ¼ cup cornstarch, and 2 tablespoons each lemon zest and fresh lemon juice. Pour onto dough in pan, top with reserved dough, and bake as directed.

Pineapple Upside-Down Cake

Makes 1 (10-inch) cake

Welcome loved ones with this classic cake; after all, pineapples and Southern hospitality go hand in hand.

Topping:
- ½ cup granulated sugar
- ¼ cup butter
- 1 (20-ounce) can pineapple slices in juice, drained and juice reserved
- 7 maraschino cherries, stemmed

Cake:
- 6 tablespoons butter, softened
- 1 cup granulated sugar
- ½ cup firmly packed light brown sugar
- 2 large eggs
- 2 cups cake flour
- 1 teaspoon baking powder
- 1 teaspoon salt
- ¾ cup whole milk
- 2 teaspoons vanilla extract

1. Preheat oven to 350°.

2. For topping: In a 10-inch cast-iron skillet, cook sugar, butter, and 3 tablespoons reserved pineapple juice over medium-low heat, stirring occasionally, until sugar is dissolved, 3 to 5 minutes. Remove from heat, and let cool for 10 minutes.

3. Arrange pineapple slices in bottom of skillet. Place a cherry in center of each pineapple slice; reserve remaining pineapple and juice for another use.

4. For cake: In a large bowl, beat butter and sugars with a mixer at medium speed until fluffy, 3 to 4 minutes, stopping to scrape bowl. Add eggs, one at a time, beating well after each addition.

5. In a medium bowl, whisk together flour, baking powder, and salt. In a small bowl, stir together milk and vanilla. Gradually add flour mixture to butter mixture alternately with milk mixture, beginning and ending with flour mixture, beating just until combined after each addition. Gently spread batter onto fruit.

6. Bake until a wooden pick inserted in center comes out clean, about 1 hour. Let cool in pan for 5 minutes. Run a knife around sides of cake, and invert onto a serving plate. Let cool for at least 30 minutes before serving.

Family Gatherings

FAMILY MEALS

Michael and I try to spend time with our children and grandchildren as much as possible. Of course, you never need a reason to visit with your loved ones, but if it's a special occasion, all the better. The following pages feature a few of my favorite menus for our family celebrations throughout the year.

Farm to Table

GETTING BACK TO OUR SOUTHERN ROOTS

Farm to table, farm to fork, seed to plate—no matter which term you use, it's obvious that cooking and eating locally grown food is something that people are really seeking out these days. Trendy as it may seem, this way of eating has always been a way of life for folks down South. I love to celebrate the harvest of the seasons by serving up nature's bounty; that's how it's always been for Southerners and how it always should be.

Farm to table is what I've always known. I don't remember eating anything that was canned unless my grandmother canned it. She would grow the beans and tomatoes and can the beans and tomatoes. Naturally that's embedded in me, and I try to stick to that.

At my home in Savannah, I grow as much as I'm capable of tending, including bell peppers, cucumbers, squash, tomatoes, eggplant, okra, and potatoes, as well as Meyer lemon and kumquat trees. My chickens provide me with fresh eggs daily for breakfast, cooking, and baking.

I'm inspired to cook by what's in season, and this meal is based on what I grow in my garden, rounded out with other produce and meats from local shops.

TABLESCAPE IDEAS

Gather pieces from around your home that have a comfortable, lived-in look. Create centerpieces using wildflowers and sunflowers. Complete the table with lanterns for ambient lighting so your crowd can visit into the evening.

Heirloom Tomato Salad with Shallot Vinaigrette

Makes 8 servings

Shallots bring a mild onion flavor to this dressing; fresh chives would also be great.

½ cup extra-virgin olive oil
¼ cup sherry vinegar
2 tablespoons minced shallot
¾ teaspoon kosher salt
⅛ teaspoon ground black pepper
5 large heirloom tomatoes, sliced ½ inch thick
1 cup thinly sliced English cucumber
¼ cup fresh tarragon leaves
Shaved ricotta salata cheese

1. In a resealable jar, combine oil, vinegar, shallot, salt, and pepper; seal jar, and shake vigorously to combine. Refrigerate for up to 5 days.
2. Arrange tomatoes and cucumber on a serving platter, and top with tarragon and cheese. Drizzle with dressing just before serving.

KITCHEN TIP

Ricotta salata is a firm, slightly salty cheese. It's available in most grocery stores, but feta cheese is a good subsitute if you can't find ricotta salata.

Summer Squash Medley

Makes 8 to 10 servings

This quick and easy side dish is perfect for any warm-weather meal.

1 cup fresh black-eyed peas
3 tablespoons unsalted butter
1½ cups chopped Vidalia onion
2 cups chopped zucchini
2 cups chopped yellow squash
1 teaspoon fresh thyme leaves
1 teaspoon kosher salt
⅛ teaspoon ground black pepper

1. In a small saucepan, bring peas and water to cover to a boil over high heat. Reduce heat, and simmer until peas are just tender, about 20 minutes. Drain.

2. In a large skillet, melt butter over medium-high heat. Add onion; cook, stirring occasionally, until translucent, about 6 minutes. Add zucchini and squash; cook, stirring occasionally, until tender, about 5 minutes. Stir in peas, thyme, salt, and pepper; cook until heated through, about 5 minutes.

Creamed Field Peas

Makes 8 servings

Like creamed corn? Give this yummy variation a try.

6 cups fresh field peas
12 slices smoked bacon, chopped
2 medium onions, chopped
3 cups heavy whipping cream
2 teaspoons kosher salt
¼ teaspoon ground black pepper

1. In a large saucepan, bring peas and water to cover to a boil over high heat. Reduce heat, and simmer until peas are tender, 20 to 30 minutes. Drain.

2. In same saucepan, cook bacon and onion over medium heat, stirring occasionally, until bacon is crisp and onion is translucent. Stir in cream, and cook until reduced by half.

3. Stir in peas, salt, and pepper; cook, stirring frequently, until peas are well coated and mixture is thick, about 10 minutes.

Peach-Stuffed Pork Loin

Makes 10 to 12 servings

Fresh fruit and pork are a classic food pairing.

1 (7-pound) pork loin, trimmed
2 quarts whole buttermilk
2½ teaspoons kosher salt, divided
2 teaspoons ground black pepper, divided
3 fresh peaches, peeled and sliced
6 tablespoons unsalted butter, softened
3 tablespoons chopped fresh thyme, divided
2 cups chicken stock
1 tablespoon Dijon mustard

1. In a large nonreactive bowl, combine pork and buttermilk. Cover and refrigerate overnight.

2. Preheat oven to 350°. Line a large rimmed baking sheet with foil; place a wire rack on top.

3. Remove pork from bowl, discarding buttermilk, and pat dry. Place pork lengthwise on a cutting board with one narrow end closest to you. Holding your knife parallel to the the longer side of the loin, make a lengthwise cut along the bottom-third of one long side, cutting to within ½ inch of other long side. Open meat at incision as if you were opening a book.

4. Again holding your knife parallel to the cutting board with the blade facing the thicker side, make another lengthwise cut into the thicker side of the loin, cutting to within ½ inch of opposite side. Open meat again at new incision. Flatten meat to an even thickness, if necessary (do not flatten any thinner than ½ inch thick).

5. Sprinkle 2 teaspoons salt and 1½ teaspoons pepper onto pork; arrange peaches, butter, and 2 tablespoons thyme lengthwise in center of pork. Starting at one long side, roll up pork and filling. Tie pork together at 1-inch intervals using kitchen string. Cut pork in half crosswise.

6. Heat a large cast-iron skillet over high heat. Cook pork pieces until golden brown, 3 to 5 minutes per side. Place pork pieces on prepared rack.

7. Bake until a meat thermometer inserted in thickest portion registers 130°, 30 to 50 minutes. Transfer pork pieces to a cutting board, and let stand for 20 minutes before slicing.

8. Meanwhile, in same skillet, cook stock over medium-high heat until reduced by half, scraping skillet with a wooden spoon to loosen any brown bits. Stir in mustard, remaining 1 tablespoon thyme, remaining ½ teaspoon salt, and remaining ½ teaspoon pepper. Serve sauce with pork.

Garden Salad with Tomato Vinaigrette

Makes 8 to 10 servings

This versatile dressing is great with any lettuce or salad green.

1 medium tomato, grated
2 tablespoons red wine vinegar
1 teaspoon kosher salt
⅛ teaspoon ground black pepper
½ cup extra-virgin olive oil
4 cups torn red leaf lettuce
4 cups torn green leaf lettuce
1 medium tomato, chopped
3 radishes, thinly sliced
3 green onions, thinly sliced
½ cup thinly sliced English cucumber
½ cup shredded or matchstick carrots
½ cup chopped mixed fresh herbs (such as basil, dill, and parsley)

1. In the container of a blender, process grated tomato, vinegar, salt, and pepper until smooth. With blender running, add oil in a slow, steady stream until well combined. Cover and refrigerate for up to 3 days.

2. In a large bowl, toss together lettuces and all remaining ingredients. Drizzle with dressing just before serving.

Roasted Herbed Potatoes

Makes 10 to 12 servings

These potatoes are crisp on the outside and tender on the inside.

6 pounds baby Yukon gold
   potatoes
3 tablespoons extra-virgin olive
   oil
2 tablespoons minced fresh
   rosemary
2 tablespoons minced fresh
   chives
2 tablespoons minced garlic
1 tablespoon kosher salt
½ teaspoon ground black
   pepper
Garnish: fresh rosemary

1. Preheat oven to 425°. Line 2 large rimmed baking sheets with foil.
2. Divide potatoes, oil, rosemary, chives, garlic, salt, and pepper
between prepared pans; toss together until well combined. Spread in
an even layer on pans.
3. Bake until potatoes are tender and lightly browned, about
30 minutes. Garnish with rosemary, if desired.

Chocolate Tart with Glazed Berries

Makes 1 (10-inch) tart

A topping of juicy berries makes a scrumptious contrast to the rich chocolate filling of this easy dessert.

½ (14.1-ounce) package
    refrigerated piecrusts
1¾ cups heavy whipping cream
1 (12-ounce) package
    semisweet chocolate morsels
1 large egg
1 egg yolk
1 teaspoon vanilla extract
½ teaspoon orange zest
⅛ teaspoon kosher salt
3 tablespoons raspberry
    preserves
1 cup fresh raspberries
1 cup fresh blueberries

1. Preheat oven to 350°.

2. Unroll piecrust, and press into bottom and up sides of a 10-inch removable-bottom tart pan; trim excess dough. Top with a piece of parchment paper, letting ends extend over edges of pan. Fill with pie weights.

3. Bake for 15 minutes. Carefully remove paper and weights, and bake 5 minutes more. Remove from oven, and let cool completely. Reduce oven temperature to 250°.

4. In a medium saucepan, cook cream and chocolate over low heat, stirring frequently, until mixture is melted and smooth. Remove from heat.

5. In a medium bowl, whisk together egg, egg yolk, vanilla, zest, and salt. Whisk chocolate mixture into egg mixture in a slow, steady stream until well combined. Pour mixture into cooled crust.

6. Bake until center is set, 40 to 50 minutes. Let cool completely in pan. Refrigerate until cold, about 2 hours.

7. Heat preserves in a medium microwave-safe bowl until melted, about 30 seconds. Gently stir in berries until coated, and spoon onto tart; serve immediately.

KITCHEN TIP

No pie weights? Use dried beans, uncooked rice, or even coins.
The beans and rice can be used repeatedly for baking but will not be edible.

Family Reunion

A SUMMER POTLUCK

Here in the South, our gatherings are usually potlucks. There's nothing we love more than bringing our favorite casserole or big-batch side dish to cookouts, church events, or neighborhood get-togethers. But one of my absolute favorite potluck occasions is a family reunion. I'm lucky enough to have my family nearby, so it's easy to gather everyone. A family reunion is a great excuse to get relatives both near and far together to catch up.

The Southern family reunion has just what you would expect: lots of family, lots of food, and lots of love. We don't do anything small in the South, and we absolutely love any excuse to throw a big bash.

There are so many ways to incorporate fun ideas into your reunion. We held our most recent reunion at my house, but there are many reunion-friendly locations if one person doesn't want to host. Check into local parks, renting a beach or lake house, or even camping if that's your style.

Ask each relative to bring a favorite dish so all the cooking doesn't fall on one person. Send out a list of what you'll need and how many of each—for example, four appetizers, two entrées, six sides, and three desserts—and let family members make their favorite dish for the category they choose. You'll get a plethora of beloved family foods. Or, send out recipe cards for inspiration and ease.

Don't forget to delegate someone to bring disposable plates, napkins, and silverware so you can spend less time cleaning up and more time with family.

A family reunion is also a great time to bring out your creative side. Design a logo for the reunion, and get it printed on T-shirts and other custom products. Assign someone to come up with fun activities and lawn games to keep the kids entertained and bonding with cousins they haven't seen in awhile.

No matter where you hold your family reunion, what games you play, or what food you eat, the most important thing is spending time with each other and having fun. And enjoying a potluck meal with delicious food doesn't hurt either!

TABLESCAPE IDEAS

Dress up folding tables with colorful linens in classic picnic colors and patterns like red gingham paired with shades of blue and bright yellow. Cheery florals mixed with greenery from the yard add a punch of color to the tables. Add labels to small paper bags to make individual flatware sets. And, craft cute food identifiers using ears of corn cut in half to hold recipe name cards.

Barbecue–Ranch Cornbread Salad

Makes 10 to 12 servings

*This flavorful layered salad can be made in stages and holds up
well in the fridge so you can make it the day before your party.*

1 cup thawed frozen lima beans

1 cup thawed frozen corn
kernels

1 cup thawed frozen black-
eyed peas

1 cup chopped red bell pepper

1 cup chopped seedless
cucumber

½ cup thinly sliced green onion

3 tablespoons chopped fresh
basil

2 tablespoons chopped fresh
parsley

1 tablespoon olive oil

1 tablespoon white wine
vinegar

1 teaspoon kosher salt

1 teaspoon ground black
pepper

2 (6-ounce) packages
cornbread mix

¼ cup butter, melted

1 large head romaine lettuce,
chopped

3 tomatoes, seeded and
chopped

1½ cups mayonnaise

1 cup vinegar-based barbecue
sauce

1 tablespoon Worcestershire
sauce

1 (1-ounce) package ranch
dressing mix

1 (16-ounce) package bacon,
chopped and cooked

1. In a large bowl, stir together lima beans, corn, black-eyed peas, bell pepper, cucumber, green onion, basil, parsley, oil, vinegar, salt, and pepper. Cover and refrigerate for up to 2 days.

2. Bake cornbread mix according to package directions for an 8-inch pan. Let cool completely.

3. Preheat oven to 400°.

4. Cut cornbread into ¾-inch cubes. On a large rimmed baking sheet, toss together cornbread cubes and melted butter until well coated; spread in a single layer.

5. Bake until golden brown and crisp, 10 to 15 minutes. Let cool completely.

6. In a large serving bowl, layer cornbread cubes, lettuce, tomatoes, and lima bean mixture.

7. In a medium bowl, whisk together mayonnaise, barbecue sauce, Worcestershire, and ranch mix; spread onto lima bean mixture, and sprinkle with bacon. Cover and refrigerate overnight before serving.

BARBECUE-RANCH
CORNBREAD SALAD

CREAMY LOA
POTATO SAL

Creamy Loaded Potato Salad

Makes 10 to 12 servings

This dish combines the best of a cold potato salad and a hot baked potato with all the fixin's.

2 tablespoons butter
2 Vidalia or other sweet onions, thinly sliced
1 (5-pound) bag red potatoes, quartered
1 cup sour cream
½ cup mayonnaise
¼ cup chopped fresh parsley
¼ cup white wine vinegar
3 tablespoons chopped fresh dill
3 tablespoons whole-grain Dijon mustard
3 tablespoons sweet pickle relish
2 teaspoons kosher salt
1 teaspoon ground black pepper
¼ teaspoon garlic powder
1 (16-ounce) package bacon, chopped and cooked
1 (8-ounce) package extra-sharp Cheddar cheese, shredded

1. In a large skillet, melt butter over medium heat. Add onion; cook, stirring frequently, until tender, about 20 minutes. Increase heat to medium-high, and cook, stirring frequently, until onions are caramel colored, about 25 minutes. Remove from heat, and let cool completely.

2. In a large Dutch oven, bring potatoes and water to cover to a boil over medium-high heat. Reduce heat, and simmer until tender, 10 to 15 minutes; drain well. Let cool for 30 minutes.

3. In a large bowl, whisk together sour cream, mayonnaise, parsley, vinegar, dill, mustard, relish, salt, pepper, and garlic powder. Stir in potatoes, onions, bacon, and cheese. Serve immediately, or cover and refrigerate for up to 2 days.

Beefy Baked Beans

Makes 10 to 12 servings

You can also cook these beans in a slow cooker on low for 4 to 5 hours or high for 2 to 3 hours.

1 pound ground chuck
1 onion, chopped
1 green bell pepper, chopped
2 (55-ounce) cans baked beans, drained
½ cup ketchup
⅓ cup dark corn syrup
3 tablespoons whole-grain Dijon mustard
3 tablespoons Worcestershire sauce
2 tablespoons chili powder

1. Preheat oven to 350°. Spray a 3½-quart baking dish with cooking spray.

2. In a large skillet, cook beef, onion, and bell pepper over medium heat until beef is browned and crumbly; drain.

3. In a large bowl, stir together beef mixture, beans, and all remaining ingredients. Spoon mixture into prepared pan, and cover with foil.

4. Bake for 30 minutes. Uncover and bake until hot and bubbly, about 30 minutes more.

Squash, Zucchini, and Tomato Casserole

Makes 10 to 12 servings

*Slice the squash and zucchini and stir together the bread crumb
mixture the day before your party to save prep time.*

6 cups thinly sliced yellow squash
6 cups thinly sliced zucchini
2 tablespoons olive oil
1 teaspoon kosher salt
2 teaspoons ground black pepper, divided
2 cups panko (Japanese bread crumbs)
1 (8-ounce) package extra-sharp white Cheddar cheese, shredded
⅓ cup thinly sliced green onion
¼ cup chopped fresh parsley
1 teaspoon garlic salt
8 plum tomatoes, thinly sliced

1. Preheat oven to 350°. Spray a 3½-quart baking dish with cooking spray.

2. In a large bowl, toss together squash, zucchini, oil, salt, and 1 teaspoon pepper.

3. In a medium bowl, stir together bread crumbs, cheese, green onion, parsley, garlic salt, and remaining 1 teaspoon pepper. Spread half of bread crumb mixture in bottom of prepared pan. Arrange squash, zucchini, and tomatoes in a spiral pattern on top of bread crumb mixture. Sprinkle remaining bread crumb mixture onto vegetables, and cover with foil.

4. Bake for 30 minutes. Uncover and bake until vegetables are tender and bread crumbs are golden brown, about 30 minutes more.

Crunchy Summer Slaw

Makes 10 to 12 servings

*If you're traveling to your reunion, toss the noodles and almonds
in the salad after you get to your location so they stay crunchy.*

²⁄₃ cup rice vinegar

¹⁄₃ cup canola oil

¼ cup soy sauce

3 tablespoons honey

1½ teaspoons garlic salt

1 teaspoon ground black
pepper

2 (3-ounce) packages ramen,
seasoning packets discarded

1 cup sliced almonds

2 (12-ounce) packages broccoli
slaw

2 (10-ounce) packages angel
hair coleslaw

1 English cucumber, halved,
seeded, and thinly sliced

1 cup thinly sliced green onion

1 cup matchstick carrots

1 cup matchstick radishes

1 cup fresh cilantro leaves

1. In a small bowl, whisk together vinegar, oil, soy sauce, honey, garlic salt, and pepper. Cover and refrigerate for up to 3 days.

2. Preheat oven to 400°.

3. Crumble ramen noodles onto a rimmed baking sheet; toss with almonds, and spread in a single layer. Bake until golden brown, about 10 minutes. Let cool completely.

4. In a large bowl, toss together noodle mixture, broccoli slaw, and all remaining ingredients. Whisk dressing well, and add to slaw mixture, tossing to combine. Serve immediately.

CRUNCHY SUMMER SLAW

PICKLED VEGETABLE
PASTA SALAD

Pickled Vegetable Pasta Salad

Makes 20 servings

Quick-pickling the veggies keeps them nice and crunchy in this side dish.

Dressing:
1½ cups distilled white vinegar
¾ cup extra-virgin olive oil
½ cup chopped fresh tarragon
¼ cup whole-grain mustard
3 cloves garlic, minced
2 tablespoons sugar
2 teaspoons kosher salt
½ teaspoon ground black pepper

Salad:
2 red bell peppers, thinly sliced
2 yellow bell peppers, thinly sliced
1 pound fresh green beans, cut into 2-inch pieces
1 (10-ounce) bag matchstick carrots
1 bunch fresh radishes, thinly sliced
1 cup thinly sliced shallots
2 jalapeños, thinly sliced
1 small head cauliflower, cut into florets and thinly sliced
8 cups distilled white vinegar
¼ cup plus 2 tablespoons kosher salt
3 tablespoons sugar
2 (16-ounce) boxes rotini, cooked according to package directions

1. For dressing: In a medium bowl, whisk together vinegar, oil, tarragon, mustard, garlic, sugar, salt, and pepper. Cover and refrigerate for up to 3 days.

2. For salad: In a large bowl, combine bell peppers, green beans, carrots, radishes, shallots, and jalapeños. Place cauliflower in a medium bowl.

3. In a large saucepan, bring vinegar, salt, and sugar to a boil over high heat, stirring until dissolved. Pour two-thirds of vinegar mixture onto bell pepper mixture and remaining vinegar mixture onto cauliflower. Let vegetables stand for 15 minutes. Drain vegetables, discarding liquid.

4. In a very large bowl, stir together vegetables, cooked pasta, and dressing until well combined. Cover and refrigerate for up to 3 days.

Oven-Baked Brisket

Makes 10 to 12 servings

This tender, juicy beef is so easy to prepare and feeds a big crowd.
The dry rub is also terrific on pork and chicken.

Sweet–Smoky Dry Rub (recipe
  follows)
1 (7-pound) beef brisket, trimmed
1 onion, thinly sliced
4 cloves garlic, peeled and halved
2 cups low-sodium beef broth
2 tablespoons Worcestershire
  sauce

1. Preheat oven to 300°. Line a large roasting pan with foil.
2. Rub Sweet–Smoky Dry Rub all over brisket. Scatter onion and garlic in prepared pan, and top with brisket. Pour broth and Worcestershire onto brisket, and cover tightly with foil.
3. Bake until brisket is very tender when pierced with a fork, 5 to 6 hours. Let stand for 15 minutes; thinly slice across the grain to serve.

Sweet–Smoky Dry Rub

Makes about ⅔ cup

2 tablespoons firmly packed light
  brown sugar
2 tablespoons smoked paprika
2 tablespoons chili powder
1 tablespoon kosher salt
1 tablespoon garlic powder
1 tablespoon onion powder
1 tablespoon ground black pepper

1. In a small bowl, whisk together all ingredients. Store in an airtight container for up to 3 months.

Baked Crescent Sandwiches

Makes about 12

You might want to make a double batch of these because grown-ups love them as much as children.

2 (8-ounce) cans refrigerated crescent dough sheets
¼ cup butter, melted
2 tablespoons whole-grain Dijon mustard
1 tablespoon Worcestershire sauce
1 (8-ounce) package sliced provolone cheese
½ pound thinly sliced deli ham
½ pound thinly sliced deli turkey
½ pound thinly sliced deli roast beef
1 (8-ounce) package sliced mozzarella cheese
Sesame seeds

1. Preheat oven to 375°. Lightly spray a 13x9-inch baking pan with cooking spray.

2. Unroll 1 can of crescent dough, and press into bottom of prepared pan. Bake for 10 minutes.

3. In a small bowl, stir together melted butter, mustard, and Worcestershire; brush half of mixture onto baked crescent crust. Layer with provolone, ham, turkey, roast beef, and mozzarella. Unroll remaining can of crescent dough on top of mozzarella. Brush remaining butter mixture onto dough, and sprinkle with sesame seeds. Cover with foil.

4. Bake for 15 minutes. Uncover and bake until golden brown, 10 to 15 minutes more. Let cool for 15 minutes; cut into squares to serve.

Pecan Praline Banana Pudding

Makes 10 to 12 servings

"The praline crumble in this pudding is so good you'll want to eat it like candy!"—Paula

Praline crumble:
1½ cups firmly packed light brown sugar
½ cup chopped pecans
½ cup unsalted butter
3 tablespoons heavy whipping cream
⅛ teaspoon kosher salt

Pudding:
1 cup granulated sugar
¾ cup firmly packed light brown sugar
½ cup all-purpose flour
½ teaspoon salt
4½ cups whole milk
8 large egg yolks
3 tablespoons butter
1 teaspoon vanilla extract
2 (11-ounce) boxes vanilla wafers
8 medium bananas, sliced
1 (16-ounce) container frozen whipped topping, thawed

Garnish: crumbled vanilla wafers

1. For praline crumble: In a small saucepan, bring all ingredients to a boil over medium heat; cook, stirring constantly, until mixture pulls away from sides of pan, about 4 minutes. Let cool completely; crumble into a small bowl. Store in an airtight container for up to 2 days.

2. For pudding: In a medium saucepan, whisk together sugars, flour, and salt. In a medium bowl, whisk together milk and egg yolks. Whisk milk mixture into sugar mixture until well combined. Cook over medium heat, whisking constantly, until mixture is very thick, about 10 minutes. Remove from heat, and whisk in butter and vanilla until melted.

3. Spoon mixture into a large bowl, and cover with plastic wrap, pressing wrap directly onto custard to prevent a skin from forming. Refrigerate until thick and cold, about 6 hours.

4. In a 13x9-inch baking dish, arrange vanilla wafers to cover bottom of pan. Top with half of bananas, half of praline crumble, and half of cold custard; repeat layers. Spread whipped topping onto custard, and arrange wafers around sides of pan. Cover and refrigerate for at least 2 hours before serving or for up to 2 days. Garnish with crumbled wafers, if desired.

Cozy Soup Supper

A HEARTY FAMILY MEAL

I love to welcome fall with a casual soup supper for my family.
It's a great time for everyone to take advantage of the cooler
temperatures, colorful skies, and spend quality time together.

Baked Pimiento
Cheese Dip,
page 237

There's no disputing that family is the most important thing to me, and I take every opportunity to spend time with my loved ones. In the fall, when my children and grandchildren have settled back into the routines of work and school, a weekend afternoon is the perfect time to get the Deen and Groover clans together for an early-evening home-cooked meal. The sunsets across our Riverbend home during this season are among the most spectacular all year.

Soup is a natural fit for serving any big crowd when temperatures cool off outside. It's definitely a favorite of mine and easy to make earlier in the day. I usually serve two kinds of soups: a chunky, spicier version for the grown-ups and a creamy, milder choice for my grandkids.

Once the soups are simmering, I turn my attention to an easy appetizer, a nice bread, and a little something sweet. All the recipes for this meal can be made ahead, so there's nothing left to do when everyone arrives but eat, visit with each other, and take in the beautiful autumn sunset.

Loaded Potato Soup

Makes about 3 quarts

This rich and creamy soup is perfect for cool nights.

6 slices thick-cut bacon, chopped
1 medium yellow onion, chopped
3 tablespoons all-purpose flour
2 (32-ounce) containers chicken broth
1 teaspoon kosher salt
½ teaspoon ground black pepper
4 pounds russet potatoes, peeled and chopped
1 cup heavy whipping cream
Sliced green onion
Shredded Cheddar cheese

1. In a large Dutch oven, cook bacon over medium heat until crisp. Remove bacon using a slotted spoon, and let drain on paper towels, reserving drippings in pot.

2. Add onion to drippings; cook, stirring occasionally, until tender, about 5 minutes. Stir in flour, and cook for 2 minutes. Whisk in broth, salt, and pepper until smooth. Stir in potatoes, and bring to a boil. Reduce heat, and simmer until potatoes are very tender and beginning to fall apart, about 25 minutes.

3. In a small bowl, whisk together cream and 1 cup hot soup liquid; stir mixture into soup, and cook for 5 minutes. Top servings with green onion, cheese, and cooked bacon.

Sausage and Sweet Potato Soup

Makes about 4 quarts

This hearty soup tastes even better the next day after the flavors have really melded together.

1 teaspoon olive oil
1½ pounds ground Italian sausage
2 cups chopped yellow onion
½ cup chopped celery
1 tablespoon minced garlic
2 pounds sweet potatoes, peeled and chopped
1 pound russet potatoes, peeled and chopped
3 (32-ounce) containers low-sodium chicken broth
1 (14.5-ounce) can fire-roasted diced tomatoes
10 sprigs fresh thyme, tied together with kitchen string
4 cups chopped kale
1 teaspoon kosher salt
½ teaspoon ground black pepper
Shredded Parmesan cheese

1. In a large Dutch oven, heat oil over medium-high heat. Add sausage; cook until browned and crumbly. Add onion, celery, and garlic; cook, stirring occasionally, until tender, about 5 minutes. Stir in all potatoes, and cook for 2 minutes. Stir in broth, tomatoes, and thyme, and bring to a boil. Reduce heat, and simmer until potatoes are tender, about 20 minutes. Stir in kale, salt, and pepper; cook until kale is just tender, about 5 minutes. Remove thyme bundle before serving. Sprinkle servings with cheese.

Buttermilk Corn Muffins
Makes 12

Yellow or white cornmeal mix works equally well in this bread; use whichever is your preference.

¼ cup all-vegetable shortening
2 cups self-rising cornmeal mix
1 tablespoon sugar
1½ cups whole buttermilk
1 large egg
¼ cup butter, melted

1. Preheat oven to 425°. Divide shortening among wells of a 12-cup muffin pan, and place in oven to preheat.
2. In a medium bowl, whisk together cornmeal mix and sugar. In a small bowl, whisk together buttermilk and egg. Stir buttermilk mixture into cornmeal mixture just until dry ingredients are moistened; stir in melted butter. Spoon batter into hot pan.
3. Bake until golden brown, about 12 minutes. Let cool in pan for 5 minutes; serve warm.

Baked Pimiento Cheese Dip
Makes about 3 cups

Warm and melty, this tangy appetizer is a great way to start any meal.

6 ounces cream cheese, softened
½ cup mayonnaise
2 cups shredded sharp Cheddar cheese
1 (4-ounce) jar diced pimientos, drained
⅓ cup sliced green onion
1 jalapeño, seeded and minced
2 tablespoons capers, drained
1 tablespoon Dijon mustard
1 tablespoon fresh lemon juice
½ teaspoon hot sauce
½ teaspoon Worcestershire sauce
⅛ teaspoon kosher salt
⅛ teaspoon ground black pepper
Toasted baguette slices

1. Preheat oven to 400°.
2. In a medium bowl, stir together cream cheese and mayonnaise until smooth. Stir in Cheddar, pimientos, green onion, jalapeño, capers, mustard, lemon juice, hot sauce, Worcestershire, salt, and pepper. Spoon mixture into a 1-quart baking dish.
3. Bake until hot and bubbly, about 20 minutes. Serve with baguette slices.

Pecan Pie Bars

Makes about 15

Buttery and crunchy, these sweet bars are a great dessert for a family dinner.

Crust:
- 1 cup unsalted butter, softened
- 1/3 cup sugar
- 1 large egg
- 1 teaspoon vanilla extract
- 2½ cups all-purpose flour
- 1 teaspoon kosher salt

Filling:
- 1 cup light corn syrup
- ½ cup cane syrup
- ½ cup firmly packed light brown sugar
- 1/3 cup all-purpose flour
- 2 teaspoons vanilla extract
- ½ teaspoon kosher salt
- 4 large eggs
- 2½ cups chopped pecans

1. Preheat oven to 350°. Line a 13x9-inch baking pan with parchment paper, letting excess extend over sides of pan.

2. For crust: In a large bowl, beat butter and sugar with a mixer at medium speed until creamy, about 2 minutes, stopping to scrape bowl. Beat in egg and vanilla. Beat in flour and salt until combined. Press mixture into bottom of prepared pan, and prick all over with a fork. Freeze for 10 minutes.

3. Bake crust until golden brown, about 25 minutes. Leave oven on.

4. Meanwhile, for filling: In a large bowl, whisk together corn syrup, cane syrup, brown sugar, flour, vanilla, salt, and eggs until smooth; stir in pecans. Pour onto hot crust.

5. Bake until center is set, about 30 minutes, loosely covering with foil to prevent excess browning, if necessary. Let cool completely in pan on a wire rack. Using excess parchment as handles, remove from pan, and cut into bars. Store in an airtight container for up to 5 days.

KITCHEN TIP

Don't cut the bars before they have completely cooled or the filling is likely to run.
Swap pecans for walnuts or use a mix of both nuts for a fun variation.

Menus Made Simple

MEAL PLANNER

When it's time to feed a crowd, whether big or small or whether for dinner at home or a fun get-together like tailgating, I always work better with a game plan. Good news—here's your plan! These six menus work for whatever the day holds for you and your loved ones.

Hearty Weekend Breakfast

Baked Eggs in Hash Brown Cups, page 12

Brown Sugar Bacon, page 5

Perfect Grits, page 8

Cinnamon Roll Biscuits, page 37

Fruit Salad with Sweet Orange Dressing, page 84

Best Brown-Bag Lunch

Paula's Chicken Salad Sandwiches, page 89

Marinated Vegetable Salad, page 119

Rosemary Cheese Straws, page 44

Giant Chocolate Chip Cookies, page 175

Easy Weeknight Dinner

Chicken Alfredo Pasta Bake, page 143

Creamed Corn, page 111

Blue Cheese and Sage Muffins, page 29

Strawberry Lime Bars, page 189

Backyard Cookout

Boiled Peanuts, page 59

Smoked Boston Butt Sandwiches, page 79

7-Layer Salad, page 91

Classic Potato Salad, page 105

Cherry Vanilla Ice Cream, page 186

Vegetable Supper

Heirloom Tomato Pie, page 122

Summer Succotash, page 114

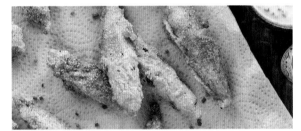

Fried Okra, page 127

Braised Collards with Country Ham, page 129

Corn Sticks, page 32

Peach Cobbler, page 165

Game Day Get-Together

Sweet and Sour Chicken Wings, page 68

Classic Deviled Eggs, page 62

Spicy Sausage Balls, page 59

Vidalia Onion Dip, page 65

Cornmeal-Crusted Fried Pickles, page 71

Mississippi Mud Brownies, page 176

Recipe Index

Coconut Sheet Cake,
page 185

PRODUCT RESOURCES

Pages 61 and 63—Southern
Rooster Round Egg Tray

Pages 192–193—Indigo Blossom
Dinnerware

Items are available through Paula's
online shop at *pauladeen.shop*
and at Paula Deen retails stores in
Savannah, Georgia; Gatlinburg
and Pigeon Forge, Tennessee; and
Myrtle Beach, South Carolina. Visit
pauladeen.com/destinations for
more information on her stores
and restaurants.

PHOTOGRAPHY CREDITS

Matt Armendariz: Front cover,
photograph of Paula Deen; viii–ix;
192; 241

Deborah Whitlaw Llewellyn:
Front cover, Perfect Pound Cake
and Southern Biscuits; Back
cover, Bacon–Pimiento Macaroni
and Cheese; iv; vii; x; xiii; xiv; 15;
25; 34–35; 39; 60–63; 86–88; 98;
116–118; 140–142; 149; 162; 170–
171; 180–181; 187, Pecan Pralines;
194–207; 208–217; 220–224; 228–
240; 254

Acknowledgements

I've always heard that it takes a village to accomplish a mission. Well, I have to say with many thanks and much love that at this moment in time I am being raised up by the most incredible village a girl could ever have, and believe me, it took a long time in the making to build this team.

Let me start by sending a big thanks to the folks here at our home. They all allow me to be free to do what I do: Patrick and Amanda Dobbs and Mike Styer. Next up, our team who mans our Savannah office: Theresa Feuger, Hollis Johnson, Cassie Powers, Melinda Rushing, Stephanie Peay, Kinzie Collett, Maria Gonzalez, and Andrew Lee. Thank y'all so much.

It goes without saying how thankful I am for the staff at The Lady and Sons and Paula Deen's Creek House in Savannah, and Paula Deen's Family Kitchen in Pigeon Forge, Tennessee, and Myrtle Beach, South Carolina. They all bring the same hospitality, love, and attention to my recipes there as I do in my home kitchen. Others that are so close to my heart are my Buffalo, New York, team headed by PDV President Steve Nanula with David Loglisci, Nick Gallegos, Anthony Nanula, and Debbie Lanoye.

Emily Warren Peterson and Mandy Russell, thank you for keeping me looking my best, along with Brenda Torre, my Minnesota magician.

I have been fortunate to have business partners who bring my ideas to life and make me proud to put my name and stamp of approval on everything we create. Universal Furniture, thank you for producing my furniture line, Paula Deen Home. Meyer produces the most beautiful and efficient cookware, bakeware, and dishware. Bob McGeeney and his design team create the most amazing small appliances, and Tiger J creates my Paula Deen clothing line. I'm grateful to Royal Academy Films for producing my TV show, *Positively Paula*. Evine, thank you for creating a home for all my products, and what fun we are having on *Sweet Home Savannah*. Thanks to Phyllis Hoffman DePiano, her sons, Brian Hart Hoffman and Eric Hoffman, and to Hoffman Media for my beautiful magazine, *Cooking with Paula Deen*. A big hug to my partner, Bob McManus, and his team in Tennessee. Bob's expertise never fails to amaze me.

Thanks to my agent, Mark Turner of Abrams Artists Agency, and to Key Group Worldwide. Jaret Keller is the best publicist I could ever have, and I can't forget P.J. These two people are definitely my Yankee family. I will always remember the fun times the three of us had in L.A. doing *Dancing with the Stars*, LOL. I send out so much love to Eddie Zorawowicz, the most incredible assistant, who most folks only dream of having. He brings calm to chaos. And a big kiss goes out to Elaine Seabolt for introducing Eddie into my world.

The ingredients for a perfect meal not only include my delicious recipes, but those who I am blessed to have at my table. My Captain Michael—best friend, love of my life, and icing on my cake—is always my dinner entertainment. My table is overflowing with love: Jamie, Brooke, Jack, and Matty; Bobby and Claudia; Michelle, Daniel, Henry, and John; Anthony, Ashley, and Bennett Rich Groover; Aunt Peggy; Bubba; Corrie and Sullivan. I am so very blessed. As we all gather around the table, we thank the good Lord for protecting us and allowing our family to grow.

PAULA DEEN®

Our Family

Paula Deen's FAMILY KITCHEN

The Lady & Sons

PAULA DEEN STORE

Paula Deen's CREEK HOUSE SEAFOOD & GRILL

PDV — PAULA DEEN VENTURES

DEEN BROTHERS

PAULA DEEN FOODS

PositivelyPaula

PAULA DEEN Home

cooking with Paula DEEN

Paula Deen's the bag lady SANDWICHES · SALADS · SWEETS

PAULA DEEN Hugs®

Visit PAULADEEN.COM

The **Bag Lady** Foundation

In 1989, after her marriage of 27 years ended in divorce, Paula was left with only $200, and money was tight while she was raising her sons Jamie and Bobby. She tried hanging wallpaper, working as a bank teller, and selling real estate and insurance. She then started a catering service, making sandwiches and meals, which her sons Jamie and Bobby delivered, and named it "The Bag Lady." Deen's home business soon outgrew her kitchen, and from there…the "Deen dream" took off. In 2012 Paula Deen established The Bag Lady Foundation.

The mission of The Bag Lady Foundation is to improve the well-being, health and independence of women, children and families, with a focus in two areas.

Nourishment
Providing food, food education and support of community efforts to feed the hungry.

Nurturing
Providing support to organizations that help women in need get back on their feet and become self-sufficient.

Of the foundation's mission, Paula says, "There is nothing worse than a child or a family going to bed hungry. And, of course, coming from where I came from, supporting the needs of single moms is something that is near and dear to my heart. I want women to feel the same kind of empowerment that has helped guide me to where I am today."

The Bag Lady Foundation receives funding through charitable contributions, as well as a portion of proceeds from Paula Deen Foods sales.

Visit thebagladyfoundation.org